THE EARTH
PLANET NUMBER THREE

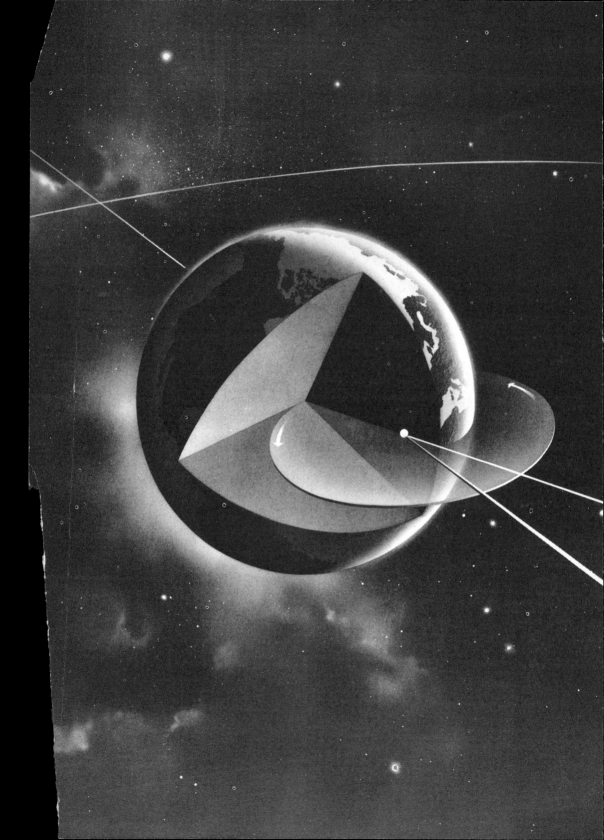

EXPLORING OUR UNIVERSE

THE
EARTH
PLANET NUMBER THREE

By FRANKLYN M. BRANLEY

Illustrated by HELMUT K. WIMMER

THOMAS Y. CROWELL COMPANY

NEW YORK

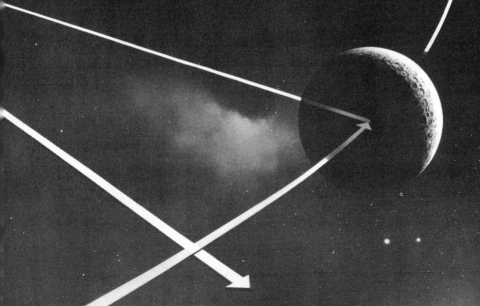

BY THE AUTHOR

Experiments in the Principles of Space Travel

Solar Energy

Exploring by Satellite: The Story of Project Vanguard

Experiments in Sky Watching

Exploring by Astronaut: The Story of Project Mercury

Exploring Our Universe

The Nine Planets

The Moon: Earth's Natural Satellite

Mars: Planet Number Four

The Sun: Star Number One

The Earth: Planet Number Three

Copyright © 1966 by Franklyn M. Branley
Illustrations copyright © 1966 by Helmut K. Wimmer

Manufactured in the United States of America
Library of Congress Catalog Card No. 66-12668
2   3   4   5   6   7   8   9   10

To Tim
of the up and coming generation

ACKNOWLEDGMENTS

I wish to thank Dr. Paul Routly, Executive Officer of the American Astronomical Society, for reading this book in manuscript and making many suggestions for its improvement.

I also wish to thank the editors of *Scientific American* for permission to adapt from their magazine the illustrations that appear on pages 71, 126, and 128. The photograph on page 35 is reproduced by the courtesy of the Mount Palomar Observatory.

CONTENTS

1

AIR, SEA, AND LAND

EARTH, PLANET number three in order of distance from the sun, is to us the most important location in the universe. Yet, compared to the size of the rest of the planets in our solar system, earth is exactly in the middle. Mercury, Venus, Mars, and Pluto are smaller; Jupiter, Saturn, Uranus, and Neptune are larger. But size is not the only criterion for measuring a planet. Of all the objects that are held in orbit by the gravitation of the sun, earth is the only one that is just the right mass to hold an atmosphere rich in both oxygen and nitrogen; it is the only one at just the right distance from the sun to have a mean temperature of about 57° Fahrenheit, which appears just right to support life; and it seems to be the only planet that has a large supply of water, a compound that is essential to life as we know it.

A few men have journeyed beyond the confines of the earth. But such excursions have been short and infrequent. Their success has depended upon man's ability to reproduce the environment he has been accustomed to on the planet itself. Man is an earthbound creature. Since his existence for millennia has been limited to the earth, man has come to think that this planet is unique in the universe and for centuries he has believed that nowhere else could creatures exist who are comparable to man. But during the past few decades his ideas have changed. Statistically it can be shown that there are hundreds of millions of possibilities within our own galaxy for the existence of planets similar to our own. And among these many planets one may logically assume there must be hundreds of thousands of places where life as we know it might have developed.

At this stage of our knowledge such fascinating possibilities are little more than conjecture. However, one need not go beyond the earth to find fascination, for this planet of ours—planet number three in the solar system—is one that astronomers, geologists, meteorologists, chemists, physicists, indeed men from scores of disciplines devote their lives to understanding. In the following pages we shall consider some of the men who have made contributions to knowledge of this planet of ours, the problems they faced and the ways they solved them, and the many problems that remain to be solved.

Essentially the earth is made of three parts—the air that blankets us, the rock and soil, the water of lakes and seas and oceans. First, let's take a look at the atmosphere.

Air

In February 1962 John Glenn, the first American astronaut to travel in an earth-circling orbit, was awed by the sight of the earth when viewed from a hundred miles above the surface.

"The view is tremendous," he said. "At this present time some clouds are visible. Sunset was beautiful. It [the sun] went down rapidly. I still have a brilliant blue band clear across the horizon, almost covering my whole window. The redness of sunset I can still see through some of the clouds way over to the left of my course. The sky above is absolutely black, completely black . . . ."

Clouds covered most of the earth, but throughout the flight Colonel Glenn could see patches of soft pastels of forests and plains, deserts and oceans. The many sunsets and sunrises that he saw were wonders of color.

The soft colors and the continual changes that an astronaut sees when viewing the earth are due to variations in the amount of water droplets and dust particles that are carried in the air. When an astronaut gets a close-up view of Mars or Venus from a space vehicle, he'll see no such beautiful sights, for the atmospheres of those planets are quite different from ours.

Of all the planets of the solar system, earth is alone in having an atmosphere that is favorable to life as we know it. The very large planets—Jupiter, Saturn, Uranus, and Neptune—all appear to have atmospheres of hydrogen. Beneath the hydrogen are deep layers of methane and ammonia, both of which are poisonous. Admittedly, knowledge of these major planets is limited; however, astronomers continue interesting researches to learn more about them. For example, in 1964 scientists from California Institute of Technology made delicate measurements of the temperature of Jupiter. They found that the temperature averages $-230°$ F. in sunlight but jumps to $-117°$ F. in the dark spots made by the shadows of its satellites. One would expect that the temperature would drop in the shadow region, but repeated experiments showed that it does rise. Two theories have been suggested to explain this apparent contradiction. One theory holds that in sunlight the atmosphere of Jupiter may be opaque. In the shadow region the substances of the atmosphere may change chemically, becoming transparent. The measuring instruments can then "see" deeper into the atmosphere, where the temperatures would be higher. Another theory suggests that in the shadow region there may be a breakdown of the molecules that permits heated materials from the deeper regions to move up to the surface in great convection currents. Obviously more observations are needed before conclusions can be reached. This is what gives zest and excitement to science—the search for answers.

Our knowledge of the small planets is limited also, but we do have some information about them. For example, Mercury appears to have no atmosphere at all. The atmosphere of Venus was probed by Mariner II and also by balloon-borne instruments. The atmosphere apparently is mostly carbon dioxide; however, a small portion of water also appears in precise spectroscopic studies carried out above the earth's atmosphere. The reason for the opaqueness of the atmosphere of Venus remains a mystery. Mars definitely has an atmosphere, although one that is much thinner than ours. The only substance identified in the atmosphere is carbon dioxide. However, it is believed that nitrogen and perhaps water vapor exist there. The amounts would be too small to show up in our instruments. The atmosphere of Pluto is unknown. The planet is some three billion miles away; a dim, small object. We should expect that its atmosphere, if it has any at all, would be made of heavy gases—the kind that a relatively small and extremely cold world might be able to retain. Chances are that whatever so-called atmosphere the planet might have would be frozen because of the tremendous distance of the planet from the energy-giving sun.

The water and dust of our atmosphere are largely responsible for sunsets, rainbows, clouds, and other effects. The amounts of these materials in our atmosphere vary a great deal from place to place because they are affected strongly by local conditions.

In addition to dust and water, the effects of which are seen easily, there are other materials in the atmosphere in varying amounts.

VARIABLE SUBSTANCES IN THE ATMOSPHERE

Water vapor	H_2O
Ozone	O_3
Ammonia	NH_3
Hydrogen sulfide	H_2S
Sulfur dioxide	SO_2
Sulfur trioxide	SO_3
Carbon monoxide	CO
Radon	Ra
Dust (soot, soil, sea salt)	—

In dry air there are certain materials, the percentage of which remains fairly constant in all parts of the world. Nitrogen and oxygen, as you will notice, make up 99 percent of the total by volume.

COMPOSITION OF THE ATMOSPHERE

Substance		Percent by Volume
Nitrogen	N_2	78.0840
Oxygen	O_2	20.9460
Argon	Ar	.9340
Carbon dioxide	CO_2	.0330
Neon	Ne	.0018
Helium	He	.0005
Krypton	Kr	.00010
Xenon	Xe	.00008
Hydrogen	H_2	.00005
Nitrous oxide	N_2O	.00005
Methane	C_2H_4	.00002

Right now each of the three billion people on the earth is breathing air no matter where he happens to be. Air is omnipresent. Not only is air everywhere around the earth but it is a very real substance. We are unaware of its weight and its pressure because, while the air pushes inward upon us, the air inside of us pushes outward. Yet a cubic foot of air weighs a bit more than one and one quarter ounces. This may not seem like much, but if one were to figure out the total number of cubic feet and multiply by the weight of each unit, he would arrive at an impressive figure. The total weight of earth's atmosphere is about $5,000,000,000,000,000$ (5×10^{15}) tons.

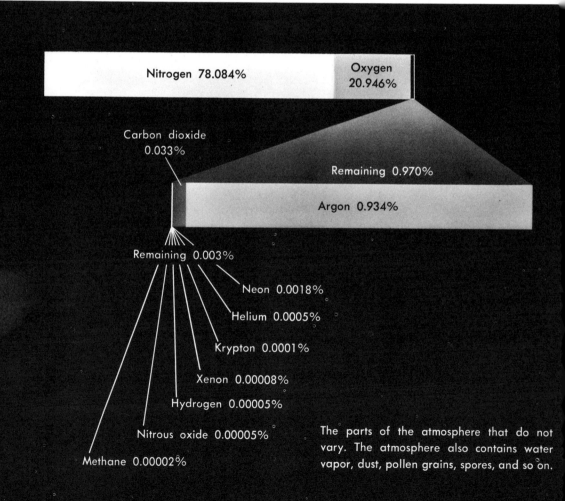

Nitrogen 78.084%

Oxygen 20.946%

Carbon dioxide 0.033%

Remaining 0.970%

Argon 0.934%

Remaining 0.003%

Neon 0.0018%

Helium 0.0005%

Krypton 0.0001%

Xenon 0.00008%

Hydrogen 0.00005%

Nitrous oxide 0.00005%

Methane 0.00002%

The parts of the atmosphere that do not vary. The atmosphere also contains water vapor, dust, pollen grains, spores, and so on.

Origin of the Air

Where did these gases come from? How did the atmosphere evolve?

According to theories of the beginning of the earth as explained in the next chapter, the atmosphere of the earth was originally composed, for the most part, of the very light gases, hydrogen and helium. In fact, more than 95 percent of the protoplanet from which earth evolved was made of these two gases. During the long, involved evolution of the earth, most of the original gases were lost, largely because of sudden flareups of the sun. Today, only small amounts of hydrogen and helium occur in the atmosphere. It is questionable if these amounts are remnants of the original atmosphere of the earth. More likely, they were released later from the solid substance of the earth, as very likely were the other gases that presently compose the atmosphere.

There was a time when earth had no atmosphere and when the sky was a deep black background against which stars shone brightly. Gases trapped in deep crevices escaped into space. Other gases were ejected by violent volcanic eruptions or bubbled to the surface of hot springs. The lighter gases may have escaped earth's gravitational attraction, but the heavier ones were held fast. Gradually the sky took on color, the myriad of colors that result when dust and other materials disperse and scatter sunlight.

Ancient volcanic eruptions account for the nitrogen in the air. They do not explain the large amount of oxygen, however, for this element is not a constituent of volcanic gases. At first small amounts of oxygen derived from water molecules. Lightning discharges in the upper atmosphere may have dissociated these molecules into hydrogen and oxygen. Even though such a process would not produce much oxygen, it probably produced enough to support the growth of primitive plants. As the plants grew, they took in carbon dioxide and released oxygen as an end product of the food-making process. As plants became larger and more numerous more and more oxygen was set free. And the more oxygen there was, the more plants could be supported. Finally the present level was reached which probably has been maintained for the past half a billion years or so.

Even though the atmosphere taken as a whole remains essentially the same century after century, changes occur within it continually. Gases are lost into outer space, and other gases are trapped in soil, rocks, and the water of the oceans. Every four to eight years the carbon dioxide of the air is renewed. The exchange of gases in the atmosphere results from an interchange between plants and animals. Carbon dioxide is continuously being used by plants. It is renewed by animals which give it out as a component of exhaled breath. When plants decay and when fires burn, the gas escapes into the air. And, as rocks weather, sediments rich in carbon dioxide are carried to the sea, where they are deposited, adding to the accumulation from the decay of plants and animals of the oceans themselves. The sea becomes the repository of carbon dioxide, holding in solution fifty times the carbon dioxide of the atmosphere.

Carbon dioxide is a basic raw material in photosynthesis. The carbon is dissociated, used in the synthesis of proteins and carbohydrates. Part of the oxygen is used in plant respiration, the rest is set free. In about three thousand years, the oxygen of the atmosphere is replaced, largely by the action of plants.

The nitrogen of the air is replenished every 100 million years, again representing a tremendous interrelationship between plants, animals, and geologic processes.

Nitrogen is a fundamental substance in proteins, basic foods of the world. Although it is the most abundant gas in the atmosphere, it is chemically inactive. It cannot be obtained readily in a form that animals and plants can use. The main agent for rendering nitrogen useful is a kind of bacteria found on the roots of certain plants. These bacteria turn nitrogen into nitrates, which dissolve in water and so can be taken in by plants. The plants are eaten by animals, and the nitrates are returned to the soil in waste products and in decaying tissue after the organism has died.

By such processes the atmosphere of the earth is changing continuously, yet remaining essentially the same, century after century, down through the eons of time.

As we move away from earth's surface we find that the air is arranged in layers, whose characteristics have been quite clearly defined by satellites. Tiros (Television Infra Red Observation Satellite) satellites have been photographing cloud cover over the entire earth. Other satellites have been probing the atmosphere at various altitudes and lead us to believe that the layers of air are not sharply separated. There are divisions in which such things as temperature and composition are uniform, but it is not easy to determine where one region ends and another one begins. Nevertheless there appear to be rather distinct layers of the atmosphere that are usually referred to as the troposphere, stratosphere, chemosphere, ionosphere, mesosphere, exosphere.

The troposphere, which extends to some 9–10 miles, contains 75 percent of all the air. It is the region within which our weather occurs. The stratosphere, immediately above, extends to about 32 miles. Beyond this region is the chemosphere. It extends to about 50 miles and is a layer in which changes occur involving the electrons of the atoms. For example, ordinary free oxygen is diatomic, made of two atoms (O_2). In the chemosphere it dissociates into monatomic oxygen (O), and then recombines. In this region water molecules are separated by solar radiation into free hydrogen (H) atoms and the incomplete hydroxyl (OH) radical, which forms water when combined with an additional hydrogen ion.

Ionization, the stripping of electrons from the outer shells of atoms, begins in the chemosphere. Above this region, and extending to some 250 miles, ionization is more severe. Solar ultraviolet radiation strips electrons violently from atoms, rendering them electrically active. Aurora displays are produced in this region by interactions of subatomic solar particles with these ions. Being electrically active, layers of the ionosphere act as mirrors, reflecting radio waves back to the earth. Indeed, our first hint that there was an ionosphere came from experiences with the behavior of radio waves back in the beginning of this century, in the days when radio was being born. On December 12, 1901, Guglielmo Marconi sent a radio message from England to Newfoundland. He was advised that the distance was too great, radio waves travel in straight lines and could not reach around the horizon. But the message was heard, so apparently somehow the waves could reach beyond the horizon. About six months later an explanation was given by Dr. A. E. Kennelly of Harvard, and a bit later by Sir Oliver Heaviside of England. They suggested that radio waves must bounce off a layer of atmosphere, much as light is reflected from a mirror.

The theory was not tested out until 1925, when the Kennelly-Heaviside layer (now called the lower part of the ionosphere) was found by aiming a radio signal upward and receiving it at a station seventeen miles away. By measuring the angles and the time, the first layer of the ionosphere was found to be at a height of 62 miles.

Further investigation has revealed that there are several distinct layers in the ionosphere, each of which reflects radio waves of different frequencies. Instruments carried in rockets and in artificial satellites have made possible investigations of the com-

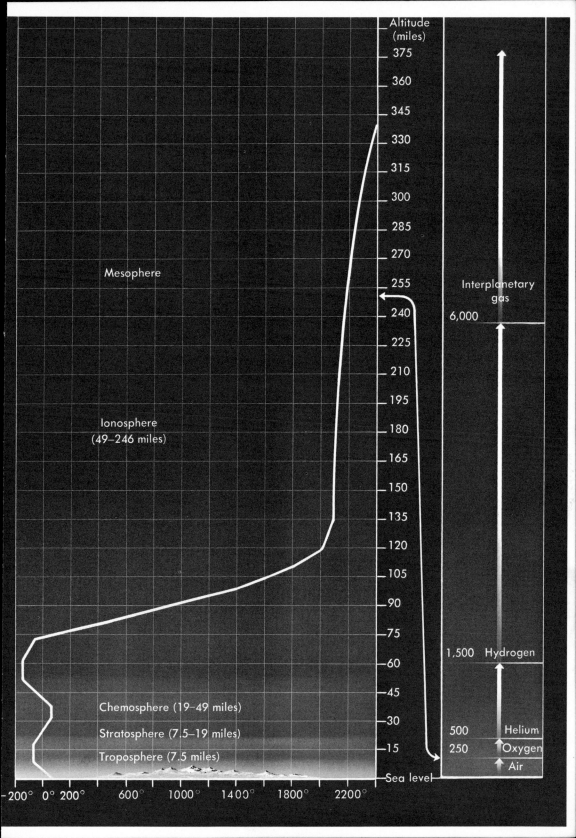

Altitude
(miles)

375

360

345

330

315

300

285

270

255

Mesophere

240

225

210

195

Ionosphere
(49–246 miles)

180

165

150

135

120

105

90

75

60

45

Chemosphere (19–49 miles)

30

Stratosphere (7.5–19 miles)

15

Troposphere (7.5 miles)

Sea level

-200° 0° 200°   600°   1000°   1400°   1800°   2200°

Interplanetary
gas

6,000

1,500   Hydrogen

500   Helium

250   Oxygen

Air

position of the air at levels up to several thousand miles. The satellite Explorer 8 showed that surrounding the earth there is a belt of helium which begins at an altitude of about 600 miles and extends to about 1,500 miles. Beyond this there appears to be a belt of hydrogen that may go as far as 6,000 miles before identity is lost and interplanetary space is reached. Admittedly, the gases in these outer belts are nebulous, nevertheless the belts are identifiable.

Later Explorer satellites probed the energy levels of various regions from 2,000 miles to some 40,000 miles. The entire area is now referred to as the magnetosphere, the region where earth's magnetic field traps and otherwise affects ionic (electrified) particles. It is the region which abounds with protons and electrons at various energy levels. Around 40,000 miles beyond the earth, the magnetic field becomes turbulent—sometimes strong, sometimes weak—always unpredictable. Scientists think this is the region where earth's magnetic field merges with fields from the sun.

One would expect that temperature would decrease steadily as he moved farther from the surface of the earth. But temperature of the atmosphere does not drop uniformly. In the lower air, up to about eight miles, temperature drops steadily, because the air is heated primarily by contact with the warm earth. In the stratosphere temperature remains about 70° below zero, then it rises steadily, reaching about 50° above zero at an elevation of some 32 miles. A layer of ozone (O_3) acts as a heat absorber, catching solar radiation. Above this level, and to about 50–60 miles, the ozone disappears and temperature drops once more, reaching about 120° below zero. As altitude increases beyond this layer temperature rises steadily, probably because of the absorption of ultraviolet radiation by ions. At 375 miles the temperature has soared to around 2,400°. However, one would not feel this temperature. The reason is that temperature is a measure of molecular motion, and it gives no information about the number of molecules involved. We feel heat because of a combination of the speed of molecules and their number. At earth's surface billions of molecules collide with us in any instant. In space, the number of molecules is small. So, even though they are moving at a velocity they would acquire if heated to 2,400° here on earth, we are not aware of their presence. In space, the main factor affecting us would be direct radiation from the sun. This would be intense. Indeed, the side of anything turned toward the sun would be heated intensely, while the side away from the sun would be unbearably cold. This is one reason why artificial satellites are rotated—to achieve an even temperature throughout the device.

The atmosphere is a buffer which is shielding the earth from those parts of solar radiation which are lethal. As the diagram on the following two pages shows, the electromagnetic radiation that leaves the sun is composed of X rays and gamma rays, ultraviolet rays, visible light rays, infrared rays, and very long heat waves. Most of the solar radiation consists of visible light and ultraviolet rays. The upper layers of the atmosphere fortunately filter out the X rays and most of the ultraviolet radiation. We say fortunately because plants and animals could not survive if they were exposed to this radiation. The ultraviolet radiation we do receive, even though the amount is small compared with that which the sun produces, is responsible for suntan which can be dangerous, even deadly, as some unfortunate people learn every summer.

The energy received at ground level is mostly in the form of visible light and infrared radiation, some of which is scattered by molecules in the upper atmosphere or reflected from dust and water droplets suspended in clouds. In the lower atmos-

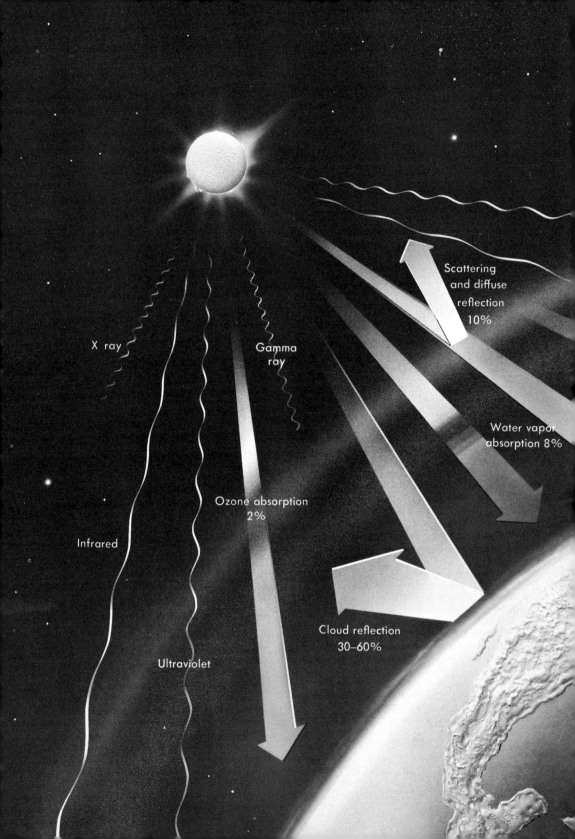

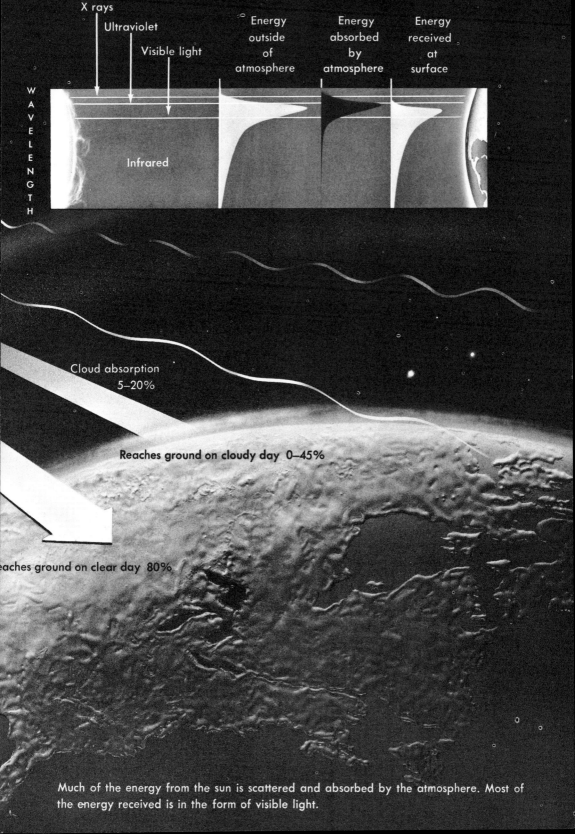

X rays

Ultraviolet

Visible light

Energy outside of atmosphere

Energy absorbed by atmosphere

Energy received at surface

W A V E L E N G T H

Infrared

Cloud absorption
5–20%

Reaches ground on cloudy day 0–45%

eaches ground on clear day 80%

Much of the energy from the sun is scattered and absorbed by the atmosphere. Most of the energy received is in the form of visible light.

phere, where the air is relatively dense, there is some direct absorption. By far the largest heating effect of the atmosphere results from the air making contact with the warm earth. While there is some reflection from the surface, a large part of the energy is absorbed by rocks, soil, and vegetation. As you can see from the diagram on pages 14–15, the amount of radiation received in the earth varies a great deal with changes in cloud cover.

Located where it is, and possessing the atmosphere that it does, earth provides in addition those conditions of temperature (57°) and pressure under which life flourishes. In these respects it is unique in the solar system.

The Sea

Seven tenths of the surface of the earth are covered by water. For convenience we often say that this surface cover is divided into five great oceans—the Atlantic and the Pacific, the Indian, the Arctic and the Antarctic—and numerous smaller seas such as the Caribbean, the Mediterranean, the South China Sea. When one looks at the seas of the earth in a way different from that which is customary he discovers that oceans are arbitrary divisions, for the seas blend together into one great body of water. The ancient Greeks called the seas *Oceanos Potamos,* the Ocean River, and they showed remarkable perception. In most places the continents break the smooth flow of one ocean into another. But there are vast expanses of ocean between Cape Horn and Antarctica where ships could sail east or west forever, never sighting land. The oceans flow into one another much as a river flows.

Samples of sea water taken at different places across the world vary quite a bit, but generally speaking we can say that some 35,000 parts of every million parts of sea water are made of the components listed in the table.

COMPONENTS OF SEA WATER

Dissolved Substance	*Parts per Million Parts of Water*
Sodium chloride (NaCl)	27,213
Magnesium chloride ($MgCl_2$)	3,807
Magnesium sulfate ($MgSO_4$)	1,658
Calcium sulfate ($CaSO_4$)	1,260
Potassium sulfate (K_2SO_4)	863
Calcium carbonate ($CaCO_3$)	123
Magnesium bromide ($MgBr_2$)	76
	35,000

But it was not always so.

Just as the beginning of the earth is far from clearly understood, so also is the origin of the waters of the earth. Quite a number of geologists believe that the water we have on earth today came from beneath earth's crust laden with poisonous and corrosive gases. It issued from volcanoes that at one time were so numerous that no appreciable expanse of solid earth was without them. Water vapor trapped inside the evolving planet was ejected through great breaks in the surface. The water vapor condensed. Heavy clouds formed and great deluges fell. But in the beginning the rains rarely reached the surface, for hot gases caused the liquid water to evaporate, to rise and to rejoin clouds that must have hung over the earth for millenia—shrouding the planet as the processes of evaporation, condensation, precipitation continued. Eventually, the earth cooled sufficiently for rains to fall upon the surface. The primal floods did not fill the basins as we know them today. More likely, only about 20 percent of the water collected at that time. But for century after century and millenium after millenium the planet continued to cool. It probably shriveled up and wrinkled the way a plum does as it becomes a prune. Stresses and strains produced new fissures, breaks in the crust grew into volcanoes. Through these new openings water vapor was thrown into the atmosphere, much of it ultimately raining down, cascading over steep cliffs and down mountainsides, wearing away sharp edges of the new-formed planet, and washing into the broad lower regions that were destined to become the ocean basins.

Its atmosphere makes earth unique among the planets. So does its water. We know that Venus contains water, and so also does Mars. Very likely we shall find that water is not a complete stranger to the major planets—Jupiter, Saturn, Uranus, and Neptune. But we can be quite certain that no planet of our solar system contains anywhere near the percentage of water that ours does. Indeed, were we being studied by scientists in some far-off location, they would dub us the planet of water. And they would know about our great expanses of water by the bright mirrorlike reflection of the sun. When observing another planet, one phenomenon the astronomer looks for is a bright reflection such as would be apparent periodically if there were bodies of water of any appreciable size on the planet.

Until a relatively short time ago, only a small part of the surface of the seas of our planet had been explored. And even as late as the early part of the last century the bottom of the sea was thought to be a fairly level plain of quite uniform depth out beyond the shelf that seemed to surround each continent. By the end of the century measurements of depth had been made, but the number was deplorably small. Soundings were made by lowering a weight at the end of a wire. Some seven thousand measurements at depths greater than a mile were made. This means that there was one measurement for every twelve thousand square miles.

In this century we learned to probe depths by reflected sound waves. As you probably know from hitting rocks together under water, sound waves travel well in water. A sound generator sends out a pulse, the sound wave travels to the bottom, is reflected, and received. The speed of sound in water is known. When this is multiplied by one half the time required for the sound to make a round trip, the depth of the water is found. Now soundings of the sea are made continually, and there are maps of the deeps and shallows in all parts of the sea all around the world.

The deep regions of the sea are far deeper than the mountains of the earth are high. If Mount Everest, the highest mountain, were placed in the deepest part of the sea, water would extend a mile above it. The deepest parts of the sea are in the Pacific Ocean basin; the great Mariana trench south and west of Guam, where the depth is 35,640 feet, and the Philippine trench just east of the islands, where the depth is 34,578 feet. The ocean is so deep and so extensive that the solid land could be fitted into it seven or eight times over. Another way of thinking about it: if the surface of the planet were smoothed off, all high and low places evened out, the earth would be entirely covered with two miles of water.

From soundings made around the world, and from first-hand observations made with bathyspheres and other deep-diving equipment, we know that the floors of the oceans differ from one another just as do the contours and topography of the continents. Yet each of the oceans has three major parts in common with the others. The continental shelves are regions of gradual change from solid land to deep water. Beyond the shelves are the continental slopes, which may extend for a hundred miles or more. These fall off rapidly to the third type of region, the deep sea floor.

During the evolution of the continents to their present shapes and sizes, the continental shelf was alternately dry land and covered by the seas. In some areas, off the west coast of the United States for example, the shelf is only about ten miles wide. In other parts of the world, as off southern Asia, the shelf slopes gradually some eight hundred miles into the sea. This is the region of the sea where plant and animal life abounds; the continental shelves are the fishing banks that supply the larder of the world with fish and clams, lobsters and shrimp—delicacies of the sea.

The continental shelves end abruptly and the hidden land falls away. Down and down it goes—8,000, 12,000, 18,000 feet. There are no plains or plateaus to interrupt the steady drop. In some regions the drop-off is over five miles, steadily downward. The surfaces of the slopes are not smooth but lined with deep canyons and fissures. Occasionally, gorges cut back into the continental shelves. At other places, broad channels extend for tens of miles along the ocean floor, fanning out like a mammoth river system. Off the Hudson River there is a vast submarine canyon that extends 150 miles into the sea, and another one is associated with the Congo. Oceanographers are hard-pressed to explain such formations. Perhaps they are canyons cut out by the rivers during eons of time when these parts of the continent were raised above ocean level. Perhaps they have grown as gigantic amounts of underwater mud and silt slid down high precipices to lower levels and were carried away by persistent deep-flowing currents.

The continental slopes fall off to the deep ocean floor—the very bottom of man's world—a place of everlasting cold and utter darkness. The floors are not flat places, as one expects a floor to be. They are cut by canyons and ridges, by island chains and mountain systems. Sediments laid down for millennia are half a mile deep, and much deeper in some places. The sediments are the remains of plant and animal life produced by the sea itself, and material eroded from the solid earth and carried into the sea by rivers and streams. Some authorities reckon that 3 billion tons of solid earth are dropped into the sea every year.

It is easy to understand why men would have reached incorrect conclusions about the sea when their knowledge was limited. They saw the level expanse of the ocean surface and experienced the gradual slope from the continents outward. Therefore it was reasonable for them to suppose that the floor of the sea sloped gradually but continually to depths beyond one's imagination. One of the greatest of surprises was the discovery of great submarine peaks that rose out of the abyssal darkness. Sometimes they towered high enough to break the surface, producing islands such as the Azores and Ascension Island. The mountains are not lone peaks usually, but rather are great mountain chains ten thousand miles from end to end and five hundred miles from side to side. The islands of the Pacific Ocean are the peaks of smaller mountain chains—often only a few hundreds of miles in extent. Just about all the mid-ocean islands are built of materials that originated in volcanoes. This is quite different from islands close to continental shores, such as Great Britain, Puerto Rico, the Dutch Antilles, which are composed of granitic rock.

Most of the geologic formations that occur beneath the sea have their land-based counterparts. However, there is one major exception. It is called the Guyot—an abrupt-rising mountain with a flat plateau-like surface. More than five hundred of them have been found in the Pacific and a hundred or so in the Atlantic. They appear to be volcanic peaks that were worn down at some time when they stood above the level of the sea. Now their plateau tops lie a half mile or so beneath the surface. Probably the entire mountain peak sank lower and lower, pressed down by its own weight.

Other unique features of submarine geology are the canyons. These are not gradual depressions, but great abrupt drop-offs, reaching down below sea level much more deeply than the mountains of earth rise above it. Curiously the great deeps of the sea lie next to high-rising mountains whose peaks thrust into the open air. Perhaps a balance is maintained, in some unknown fashion, between up-thrust and fall-off—one matched against the other. The deeps of the great ocean canyons shroud many mysteries. Man's efforts to probe the areas are seriously hampered by the stupendous pressures that exist there (seven tons to a square inch in some places), by the stiffening cold, and by the complete darkness.

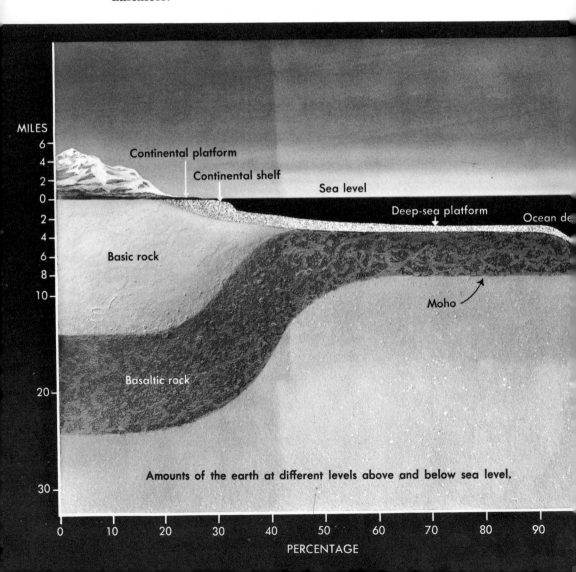

Amounts of the earth at different levels above and below sea level.

The Land

Similarly, except for a thin section of the outer crust, man is unable to explore first hand the solid part of the earth. Yet by using the skills and techniques of seismology, the science of earthquakes, he has considerable knowledge of the surface and depths of this planet on which we live.

Much more of the surface of the earth is under water than above it. Only 29 percent of the surface is dry land. Most of this is the continental platform.

The earth is contained within a rather rigid, solid shell that has an average thickness of only twenty miles. This shell is thinner in relation to the whole earth than the skin of an apple is to the apple itself. We believe that the crust of solid material is twenty miles thick because at that level temperature reaches 1,000° centigrade. This is high enough to cause rock to deform. Also, as explained below, this is the divider above which earthquake surface waves move rapidly.

We know that the primary rocks of the earth, those that formed from the original molten material, fall into two main groups. There are the "sialic" rocks, those that contain considerable silicon and aluminum, and the "mafic" rocks, those that are rich in magnesium and iron. Granite, which is primarily a crustal rock, is sialic; while basalt, a rock that is deeper below the surface, is mafic.

In a laboratory, waves similar in nature to the waves made by an earthquake are passed through various rock samples. In every case the waves travel faster through basalt than through granite. From repeated observations seismologists know that the speed of earthquake waves is greater in the lower part of the earth's crust than in the upper parts. This would mean the deeper parts are made of basalt, and that granite overlies the basalt. Extensive areas of the floor of the ocean appear to contain no granite at all.

The boundary of the crust, the division below which lies the mantle of the earth, is now called the Mohorovicic discontinuity, or more simply the Moho, after A. Mohorovicic, a Yugoslavian seismologist who discovered the division during an earthquake in 1909.

Every year, a dozen or so earthquakes occur. The smallest of them releases a thousand times more energy than a nuclear bomb. Earthquakes shake the earth and produce waves that travel in all directions and through both the solid and liquid parts of the earth. The primary (P) waves are compression-expansion waves like those of sound. You might think of them as push and pull. There are secondary (S) waves that vibrate up and down and at right angles to the direction in which the wave travels, much as do light waves. You might think of these as "shake" waves. The P waves travel through the liquid part of the earth as well as the solid. The S waves travel only through the solid portions, and more slowly than the P waves.

In addition, earthquakes generate waves in the surface of the planet which in many respects are similar to waves on the ocean. The waves are extremely weak, and they die out very quickly as depth increases.

Earthquake waves are picked up and registered by seismographs. These instruments may take many different forms, but the principle of their operation is explained below. A heavy mass of metal is suspended from a spring, and extending from the mass is a magnet that is free to move inside wire coils. When there is an earthquake, the coils move ever so slightly. However, the motion is enough to produce a small electric current in the coils. The electric current may be magnified and recorded so it can be read and interpreted.

The small electric current is led to a galvanometer, a current-

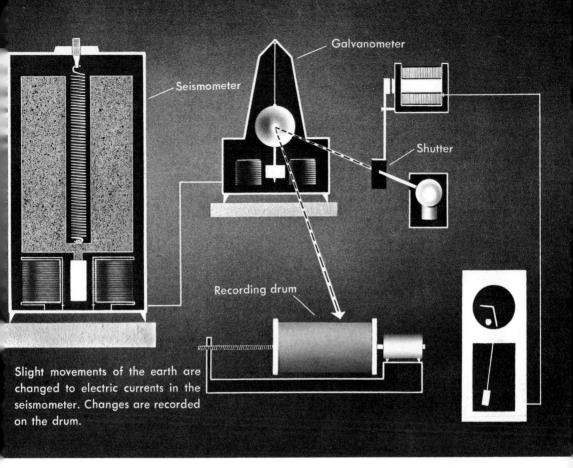

Galvanometer

Seismometer

Shutter

Recording drum

Slight movements of the earth are changed to electric currents in the seismometer. Changes are recorded on the drum.

detecting apparatus. When the current enters the galvanometer, the mirror moves—the amount of motion depending upon the amount of current. As the mirror moves it reflects a light beam (from an outside source) onto a film that is fastened to a rotating drum. A small movement of the mirror causes a large movement of the light beam. The seismologist needs one more bit of information—the time the wave was received. Once every minute a clock activates a mechanism that closes a shutter, cutting off the beam of light and producing breaks in the trace on the drum. The breaks enable the scientist to determine the moment when a particular wave reached the instrument.

By analyzing seismograms geologists have learned a great deal about the deep interior of the earth. If the earth were solid throughout, both *P* and *S* waves would travel in all directions through the core and the waves could be picked up directly opposite the place where the quake occurred. But it was found that there was a shadow region directly opposite the earthquakes, a region where no *S* waves are noted. There must be some reason why these waves cannot travel through the core of the earth. It is known that *S*, or shake, waves cannot pass through a liquid, so it is logical to conclude that there must be a liquid in the central region of the earth, in contrast to the surrounding area that is solid, or somewhat elastic.

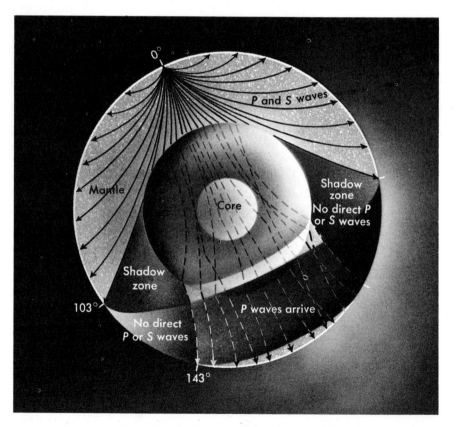

Since *P* waves are refracted when passing through earth's core and *S* waves are deflected by the core, a shadow zone which receives no direct waves results.

By careful determination of the extent of the shadow zone, seismologists have figured out that the core of the earth has a radius of 2,156 miles. The boundary of the core of the earth is rather sharply defined because *P* waves are bent sharply, and also slowed down. It appears that the outer part of the core is made of liquid iron at high temperatures and under pressure some 2 million times greater than the pressure of the atmosphere. Rather recent evidence indicates that the very center of the core, a region some 1,600 miles in diameter, behaves as though it were solid, and not liquid as seems to be the case in the outer core.

Tangible evidence of what the interior of the earth may be like is obtained by studying meteorites that originate at places

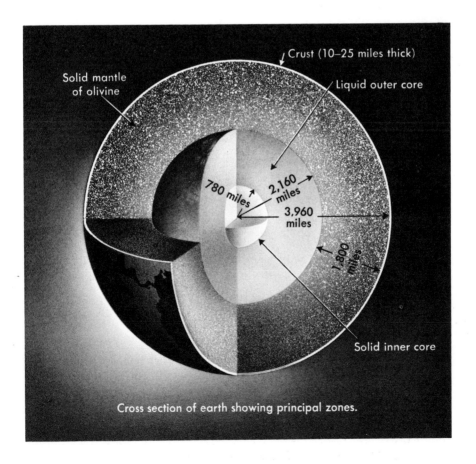

Cross section of earth showing principal zones.

far removed from our own planet. These rare objects that land on the earth may be the remains of a planet that once existed and which shattered violently a long time ago. If so, analysis of meteorites provides evidence of the structure of that planet. Assuming that all planets of the solar system had a similar origin we can then further assume that the mantle and core of our own planet have the same structure.

Meteorites occur in three main classes: the irons, the stony meteorites, and those that are a mixture of stone and iron. Stony meteorites contain mostly materials that are rich in iron and magnesium silicates. These are the same substances that compose the basic rocks of the earth. Iron meteorites are made almost entirely of an alloy of nickel and iron, and careful study of the crystals indicates that the material cooled very slowly. Stony-iron are mixtures of both of the above—nickel-iron and silicates. It would seem that meteorites once composed a planet which had an outer core of nickel-iron and which cooled very slowly, and a mantle of basalt-type rock. These are exactly the same materials which we believe are contained in the outer core and mantle of the earth.

The temperature at the center of the earth must be extremely high, though not as high as measurements near the surface might imply. Measurements in deep mines and bore holes for oil wells indicate that temperature increases 1° F. for every 50 feet of descent, or about 100° F. per mile. If we were to follow through this reasoning to the center of the earth, the temperature there would be 400,000° F. Such a temperature is not at all reasonable. It is expected that the rate of increase experienced near the surface does not continue to earth's center. Also some of the surface heat of the earth may be due to nuclear breakdown processes that do not prevail at great depths. The best that one can do is to estimate what the temperatures might be.

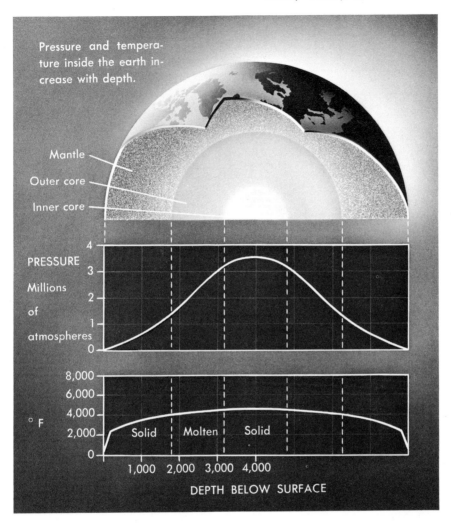

Pressure and temperature inside the earth increase with depth.

Mantle

Outer core

Inner core

PRESSURE

Millions

of

atmospheres

4
3
2
1
0

8,000
6,000
4,000
2,000
0

° F

Solid | Molten | Solid

1,000   2,000   3,000   4,000

DEPTH BELOW SURFACE

Living on the earth as we do, one would think we would know a great deal about this planet of ours. And we do. However, three big questions are a long way from being answered completely: How did the earth evolve to its present condition? How old is the earth? and What will ultimately happen to it? Suggestions about all three matters are given in the next chapter.

2

AGE OF THE EARTH: BEGINNING AND END

GEOLOGISTS HAVE determined the structure of the crust of the earth, oceanographers know the composition of the oceans, meteorologists have extensive information about the makeup and the movements of the atmosphere of the earth. These scientists have been able to assemble facts because they can make direct, firsthand observations and measurements. But when the age of the earth, its beginnings, and its future are considered, scientists must be content with only partial answers. However, facts and measurements, limited as they are, do enable scientists to formulate theories about such matters.

We can be certain that the earth is not the same today as it was yesterday. But we cannot be sure of the extent and variety of the changes that have transpired through the ages, nor the forces that might have produced the changes. Considerable research is needed to gather facts that can be used to provide reliable explanations for the formation of the earth, the other planets, and the sun. Until we have those facts, the best we can do is work out reasonable theories which fit the facts as they are known right now. One of the facts that any theory explaining the origin of the sun and its planets must consider is this: the planes of the orbits of all the planets are essentially the same as that of the earth. To visualize the plane of earth's orbit you might imagine a round tabletop with the sun at the center and the earth moving around the edge. The surface of the table would be the plane of earth's orbit. The orbits of most of the satellites of the planets are only slightly inclined to the same plane. For example, the moon's orbit is inclined only 5 degrees to the plane of earth's orbit.

All of the planets go around the sun in the same direction— counterclockwise when observed from above the North Pole. With only a few exceptions, the satellites go around the planets in the same way. The planets rotate in the same direction, with the exception of Uranus and Venus. Altogether, some sixteen hundred motions are recognized in the solar system. Of these, less than two dozen do not fit the pattern of motions.

The planets are not situated at random distances from the sun. Johann Daniel Titius of Wittenberg, in 1772, announced a rule based upon observation and not, therefore, a truly mathematical rule for representing the proportional distances of the planets from the sun. This rule was given popularity a few years later by Johann Elert Bode (1747–1826), a German astronomer who was at one time director of the Berlin Observatory. The rule became known as Bode's Law, even though Bode did not originate it, and even though the rule really is not a law at all.

According to Bode's Law, the proportional distances of the planets from the sun are obtained by adding 4 to the series of numbers 0, 3, 6, 12, 24, 48, 96, 192, 384, 768. When the results are multiplied by 10 you have the distances to the planets in millions of miles, as shown on the following page.

Planet	Bode's Series plus 4			Actual Distance (Millions of miles)
Mercury	0 + 4	× 10	40	36
Venus	3 + 4	× "	70	67
Earth	6 + 4	× "	100	93
Mars	12 + 4	× "	160	141
Asteroids	24 + 4	× "	280	290
Jupiter	48 + 4	× "	520	483
Saturn	96 + 4	× "	1,000	886
Uranus	192 + 4	× "	1,960	1,783
Neptune	384 + 4	× "	3,880	2,791
Pluto	768 + 4	× "	7,720	3,671

Whether or not this rule has any validity we cannot say. However, it does point out that distances from one planet to another are doubled in many instances. For example, the distance from the sun to the asteroids (290 million miles) is just about twice the distance from the sun to Mars, Saturn is twice the distance to Jupiter, and Uranus is twice the distance to Saturn. The rule breaks down when you consider Neptune and Pluto.

This approach to the distribution of the planets may have no significance at all. However, there are other theories to explain the distribution which we will discuss later.

Origin of the Earth

About two hundred years ago, the German philosopher and teacher Immanuel Kant (1724–1804) proposed a theory of the origin of the planets that seemed to fit all the requirements. He said that the sun and planets evolved from a great nebula—a mist or cloud. Around the end of the eighteenth century, the French mathematician and astronomer Pierre Simon de Laplace expanded Kant's theory, but he supported the basic Kant idea. The theory was known as the Nebular Hypothesis. Certain aspects of this early conception of the origin of the solar system are still retained. Several physicists and astronomers have made other suggestions. Some said that another star approached close to the sun, and each pulled great masses of gas from the other. The gases congealed to form planets and satellites. Others have suggested that the sun used to have a companion star. A third star came in close to the pair, stealing away the sun's companion. In the process gases were pulled from all three stars and set free in space. The gases packed together to become planets. There are scientists who believe our sun and the planets were formed from debris produced by the explosion of many supernovas, extremely energetic and explosive stars—a cataclysm of cosmic proportions.

The visiting star idea has many drawbacks. One basic weakness concerns the number of planetary systems believed to exist. The distances between stars is tremendous. For example, in a sphere some thirty light-years across with the sun at the center, there are only about forty stars. We would expect that close approaches of two stars would, therefore, be extremely rare. If planets were formed from gases that were pulled out from stars during such close approaches, then we should expect planets to be extremely rare. Just the opposite appears to be the case.

Outside of our own solar system there must be millions of similar formations. We know positively of only one other planet; the one that is called Barnard B. In 1916 the American astronomer E. E. Barnard discovered that a dim star in the constellation Ophiuchus was moving very rapidly northward. In about 180 years it moves as much as the diameter of the moon, about one half degree. Also, the star was close to the earth; only the triple-star Alpha Centauri was closer. In 1963 Peter van de Kamp of Swarthmore College announced the completion of a study of the side-to-side motion of Barnard's star as it moved across the sky. After he and his associates had studied 2,415 photographs, made over a period of about twenty-five years, it was concluded that the star's motion was being affected by the gravitational attraction of an unseen companion. The mass of the companion was found to be a small fraction of the star itself, only about 1.5 times the mass of Jupiter. The average distance separating the two objects is about four times the distance between the earth and the sun. This means that the companion must be defined as a planet. In order for a collection of material to be a star, the mass must be great enough to maintain a high central temperature. The temperature must be enough to initiate nuclear reactions that change hydrogen into helium. Astronomers know that Barnard B has insufficient mass to be a star. It is a cold body reflecting light that is given off by Barnard's star. It is far too dim to be detected by any apparatus here on the earth. However, we can be certain of its presence.

Companions affecting the motions of other stars have also been discovered. In 1943 Kaj Aa Strand found that a companion was affecting motions of the star 61 Cygni. In 1960 Sarah Lee Lippincott found that the star Lalande 21185 was moving back and forth because of a nearby companion. However, both these companions were considerably more massive than Barnard B; too massive to be classified as planets.

Astronomers generally believe that were it possible to gather similar data about other stars, we should find that the motions of many of them are being affected by the gravitation of rather small masses, masses that would come under the category of planets. It is believed that at least one star in a thousand, and perhaps one in a hundred, may support a planetary system. The number of stars in our galaxy can reasonably be set at around 100 billion. This would mean that at least 100 million of these stars have planets associated with them.

Because planets do not appear to be rarities in the universe, some explanation other than a visiting star must be found for their occurrence. Whatever explanation is suggested, the theory must not consider the planets alone, but it must also provide an explanation for the origin of the central star of the system itself. In our case, of course, this central star is the sun.

Our galaxy is made mostly of stars. About 95 percent of the mass of the galaxy is stellar, and the remaining fraction is composed of interstellar gases including nebulae. Many years ago, astronomers observed great black spots in front of some of these gaseous formations. Careful analysis of the spots, which are probably vast formations of partially compacted dust and gas, indicated that the spots have a mass about equal to the sun, and the distances between them are about the same as the distances between the sun and nearby stars. We can assume that these globules are protostars, stars at an early stage of formation. Even-

The nebula NGC 6611 in red light. Small dark specks are condensations of gases.

tually, we should expect the masses to be pushed closer together by the light of nearby stars. Once the gases have been compressed to a certain critical amount, gravity of the system would cause the gases to collapse. Temperature in the interior would rapidly reach several million degrees, sufficient for nuclear reactions to be initiated and the internal pressure to become high enough to prevent further collapse. In such fashion the sun may have come into existence.

An extension of this theory for the origin of the sun can be made logically to include the origin of the earth, the other planets, and their satellites. Here in brief form are the steps that may have occurred as the solar system evolved. The planets arose from the same material that gave birth to the sun. The mass was probably somewhat spherical, and had a diameter of some 10 billion miles. Most of these gases became the sun. The entire system contracted to a small fraction of the original diameter. Collapse continued as the system spun, causing the matter to form into a great flat disk. The size of the system had shrunk to a diameter of about 6 billion miles, and the thickness of the disk was in the order of one million miles.

The dust and gases in the disk churned about. Eddies formed here and there and as time passed the eddies covered less and less volume; their density increased. Most often, great upheavals within the system would break up the eddies. But occasionally an eddy became dense enough, and its own gravitational force strong enough, for the sub-system to hold together. This was the first of the protoplanets, a mass gradually compressing as it moved about the central and much larger mass, sweeping up additional dust and gas. Other protoplanets formed. Those that were at the same distance from the center of the mass joined together. As the mass changed, the orbit changed from an elongated ellipse to one more closely approaching a circle.

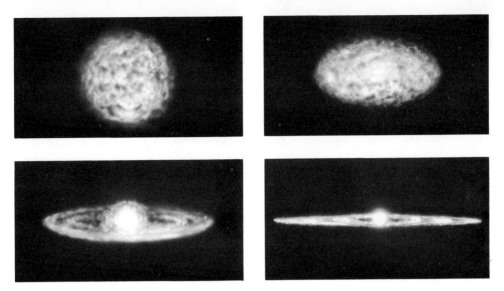

Stages in the contraction of a vast nebula, resulting in formation of a star, and possibly planets.

The primeval sun was cool. Even had it been giving out considerable energy, the early planets would have received only a small fraction of the energy, if any, because of the pall of dust and gases that lay between them and the sun. Protoplanets were cold, and so gaseous molecules condensed into ice crystals of water, ammonia, methane, and other substances. At the beginning, protoplanets were extremely sunlike, some 99 percent hydrogen and helium. As the protoplanet contracted, the denser elements sank to the center of the mass. Ices and silicates of various kinds provided a cover for the dense substances, and surrounding the whole was a vast envelope of the light gases. At some stage there might have been a tremendous flare-up of the sun causing the gases in the atmosphere of the early planets to be dissipated. At the same time, materials that evaporate quickly and which were in the crust of the primitive earth might have been evaporated. The present atmosphere would have been formed by combinations of components that emerged from the crust after the flare-up.

During the first few million years the protoplanets were so massive that they moved with regard to the sun much as the earth-moon system moves today. That is, the protoplanets made a single rotation while making a single revolution around the sun. As the protoplanets shrank in size, they rotated more rapidly. The more rapid motion is certainly apparent in the earth today, and even more marked in the major planets. They have rotation periods that range from 9 hours 50 minutes for Jupiter to close to 14 hours for Neptune.

In the great nebula that was the spawning place of the sun, density varied from one region to another. The regions of greatest density were the same as those regions which today are occupied by planets. Near the sun we expect that the strong gravitational attraction would have pulled in the gases, or the great pressure of radiation would have pushed gases away. In either case density would have been diminished in the area. The inner planets were kept small because of the sun's gravitational force, and also because the amount of building material was relatively scarce. Density would have increased with distance, reaching the highest level around Jupiter and Saturn. Beyond this area, density would have decreased outward some three billion miles or so.

During the millions of years that the protoplanets were coalescing into planets, the protosun was contracting. After some 100 million years compression of the gases had raised the temperature high enough to initiate nuclear reactions, in which hydrogen was converted to helium and great amounts of energy were produced. The sun had matured into a full-fledged star, much the same as it is today.

In its formative stages our planet lost all but about one thousandth of the material that composed the protoplanet. Hydrogen and helium, the lightest elements, accounted for most of the loss. Therefore, even though both the earth and sun originated from the same material, earth now has a much smaller percentage of these two light gases than does the sun.

For such a theory to have validity, certain observed facts must be explained. For example, if the sun formed from a nebula, a vast formation of gases, it should be spinning around hundreds of times faster than it now spins. The British astronomer Fred Hoyle, as well as other cosmogonists, has offered explanations.

The gases in a nebula are extremely thin. They are so rarified that, in order to contain all the material now in the sun, the nebula would have to have a diameter of some 10,000,000,000,-000 miles—almost two light-years. The diameter of the sun is presently about one million miles. Therefore, the gases shrank to one ten-millionth of the original size.

When a volume of gas shrinks, it must rotate. The greater the shrinkage, the faster the rotation. If the gases that made the sun shrank to one ten-millionth of the original size, then the rotation would have increased ten million times. If the original motion in the gases was only half an inch a second, the sun would now be spinning so fast that it would complete a rotation in half a day instead of in twenty-six days.

What could have happened to slow down such a tremendous gaseous mass?

Probably when the gases had shrunk to a diameter of about 75 million miles the spinning caused the spherical mass to become flattened at the poles. The mass gradually became disk-shaped. Now there began a steady flow of rotational momentum from the central core to the disk. The total angular momentum (M) is equal to the mass of the system (m) times the velocity (v) times the distance (d), or $M = mvd$. It means that a rotating body spins faster as it shrinks, but slower if it expands. The flattening of the solar sphere to a disk effectively increased the distance. When distance increased, velocity decreased. The sun was slowed down to its present speed. Also, the gases in the disk were pushed away from the central mass that was to become the sun. The gases pushed out were to become the planets. Since most of the gases were pushed far out, the location of the major planets is explained.

If the slowing down of the sun and the pushing out of material account for the present speed of rotation of the sun, then the sun ought to rotate rapidly if all the material of the solar system were to be combined in the sun. If the explanation works one way, then it should work in reverse. And it does. The sun would rotate faster, but not fast enough to fit the theory.

All the material now in the solar system does not add up to enough mass to cause the sun to spin fast enough to form a disk and slow down as explained above. Then the only thing we can conclude is that there used to be more material in the solar system than there is now. During the evolution of the sun and the planets large amounts of gases, mostly hydrogen, must have escaped from the sun's gravitational attraction and gone off into interstellar space.

From observations we can conclude that this really did occur. Jupiter and Saturn are rich in hydrogen, containing essentially the same relative amount as the sun. But Uranus and Neptune, located farther from the sun where gravitational pull is less, lack hydrogen. The gas could not be retained in the system and so escaped. The amount of gas involved was considerable, some seven times greater than the present mass of all the planets together.

If this amount of material plus the material now in the planets were to be put into the sun we would find the results would fit the theory. The sun would rotate at high speed, certainly high enough to cause a disk to develop and so result in a distribution of angular momentum.

The theory for the formation of the earth mentioned above must overcome another hurdle. After a disk developed around the gaseous condensation, the central region continued to shrink. At the same time the material in the disk was pushed farther away. It was inevitable that a separation should develop between the core of material and the inner edge of the disk.

Perhaps, as has been suggested, rotational momentum was transmitted by a magnetic field. The lines of force from the central core were stretching, so to speak, and dragging the disk material. The condensation might be thought of as the hub of a wheel connected to the outer part of the disk by spokes. When the spokes are firm and solid (inelastic), the rim of the wheel must rotate in the same period of time as the hub. But if the spokes have some give to them (elastic lines of force), the rim of the wheel could lag behind the hub. Such a stretching of the "elastic" spokes would tend to slow down the hub (the sun).

Any theory of cosmogony, the origin of things, must also explain the make-up of the planets. The inner planets are made mostly of iron and rock, materials that were only a small fraction of the original solar material. What could have happened to the substances, especially hydrogen, originally contained in the inner planets—Mercury, Venus, Earth, and Mars?

The magnetic coupling of the central mass and the disk mentioned above operates only when the materials are gaseous. Solid or liquid globules that condensed out of the gases would be unaffected by the magnetic field. They would be left behind, even though only a few yards across, while the lighter gases would continue to be pushed farther away.

The kinds of materials that could condense out of the gases would be determined by temperature for the most part. Close to the sun, where temperature would be fairly high, iron and silicates would be most apt to condense. Farther away from the sun, where the temperature is cooler, materials with lower boiling points, such as water and ammonia, would condense.

If the above process did occur, and globules of iron and silicates condensed out of the solar disk, what could have held the chunks of material together? Sticking substances have been suggested. Some people believe that water was the "glue"; others say that oil was the agent. Still others are of the opinion that pitch might have been the adhesive. Fred Hoyle thinks that the placement of the planets was not haphazard. Rather, he believes the planets formed at those locations where pitch might have been present and may have coated the globules. When they collided in the cataclysm of creation, the pitch may have bonded one mass to another, thus building a planet after multitudes of collisions and eons of time.

The search to find clues to explain the origin of the earth remains an intriguing occupation of astronomers, geologists, chemists, scientists of other disciplines, and curious laymen. We may never find the full answer. Or we may find significant clues as man moves outside the limitations of this world on which we live.

Age of the Earth

Until fairly recently the determination of the age of the earth was just as much a dead end as the search for the earth's origin. But today we are much closer to an answer.

One cannot say with any degree of exactness how long ago the material of which the earth is made was a vast, disorganized formation of dust and gases. Neither can we be certain about the time needed for these gases to contract, condense, and assume the characteristics of a planet. Before the eighteenth century, estimates of the age of the earth were regulated by restrictions of theology. The Old Testament was considered to be a history of the world, and many church people strengthened that belief by their own statements. In 1642 John Lightfoot, a scholar and administrator of Cambridge University, announced that the moment of creation was nine o'clock in the morning on September seventeenth in the year 3928 B.C.

Later, in 1658, Archbishop Ussher, Primate of Ireland, wrote:

> In the beginning God created heaven and earth, Gen. I, V. 1., which beginning of time, according to our chronologie, fell upon the entrance of night preceding the twenty third day of Octob. in the year of the Julian Calendar, 710.

Some fifty years later, Bishop Lloyd of England inserted the year 4064 B.C. in his commentary on Archbishop Ussher's statement. For more than a century the church accepted and taught that the earth began at that time. Anyone who taught otherwise was accused of heresy.

In the eighteenth and nineteenth centuries geologists began to study rocks, and from their findings began to speak of the earth's age in terms of millions, even billions of years.

At the turn of the century scientists knew that radioactive elements broke down into helium and lead in a certain period of time. In 1913 rocks were dated by the "radioactive" method. They were found to be about one billion years old.

Dating by the radioactive method works like this: The atoms of certain elements are unstable, unable to hold together. They break down and give off alpha particles (the nuclei of helium), beta particles (electrons), and gamma rays. Other radioactive atoms may be produced. These atoms, in turn, break down until stable atoms are reached. Often these atoms are lead and helium.

All the atoms of a given element are not the same. They all have the same number of protons, but they will have different numbers of neutrons. The different atoms of an element are called isotopes—thus we have uranium 238, uranium 235, uranium 233, uranium 236. Some of these, and other isotopes as well, are naturally radioactive. These might be the products of the breakdown of uranium or thorium, or products resulting from nuclear reactions caused when cosmic particles collide with certain atomic nuclei. More important for purposes of dating the earth are the primary radioactive isotopes (radioisotopes)—those formed when the elements originated. Some of these are uranium 235 and 238, thorium 232, potassium 40, and rubidium 87. All of these isotopes have long half-lives—a long time is needed for one half of a given number of them to break down. For example, the half-life of the shortest, uranium 235, is 710 million years.

Since we know how long it takes an isotope to break down, and we know the products that are formed, we have clues for finding the age of rocks. Each year and every year a small part of any mass of uranium is converted into lead 206 and helium 4. The part converted into lead is 1.5×10^{-10}, or .00000000015 of the whole. This means that as the years go by the amount of lead in any piece of uranium ore will slowly increase. We are not especially interested in the helium, for a large part escapes into the atmosphere. The changes that occur and the time required to make the changes are tabulated below.

Time (Billions of Years)	Percent by Weight		
	Uranium 238	Lead 206	Helium 4
0	100	0	0
1	86.5	12	1.5
2	75	22	3
3	65	30	5
5	50	43	7
(infinity)	00	86.5	13.5

Knowing how long it takes lead to accumulate in a sample of rock, the scientist can measure its age. All he need do is determine the relative amounts of uranium, lead, and helium. For example, some ratios and ages in millions of years are given below:

When the ratio of Lead 206 to Uranium 238 is	Age of sample in millions of years is
.08	500
.166	1,000
.36	2,000

The age of rocks found in Southern Rhodesia was computed to be 2.7 billion years. So the earth must be at least that old.

To find the greatest possible age of the earth lead deposits have been studied to determine the ratio of one kind of lead isotope to another. The minimum age of the earth then appears to be a bit over three billion years, and the maximum age is 5.6 billion years.

Aside from the crust of the earth itself, we can get indications of the age of the earth from meteorites—assuming that the earth and meteorites had a common origin. Meteorites are believed to be remnants of minor planets—objects some sixty miles or so across—that occupy the space between the planets Mars and Jupiter. Their structure indicates that they were made in a fashion somewhat like the following. The materials of which they were made packed tightly together and temperature went high enough to cause melting. The iron in the mixture separated from the stony material, and sank to the center of the mass, pulled by gravitation. Gradually the entire mass cooled. As it cooled, crystals of the different materials formed. Later the minor planets were broken up by violent collisions. The remnants of the crashes

History of the earth in billions of years: 6—upper limit for age of elements; 5.6—maximum age of earth; 4.9—minimum age of elements (possible age of solar system); 4.55—most probable age of solar system; 3.2—minimum age of earth; 2.7—age of oldest accurately dated rocks; 0.5—beginning of fossil record.

were chondrules, bits of metal, and fragments of crystals. Later on these materials were consolidated into chondrites, the most common kind of meteorite.

The dating of the events discussed above can be determined by measurements of various radioactive substances. The radium-lead process of dating gives the approximate time when the metals in meteorites separated from the stony material by the process of melting. It figures out to be around 4.5 billion years ago. A second process used in indicating years elapsed since meteorites formed employs the relative abundance of a strontium isotope that forms from the breakdown of rubidium. We think it gives the time that has passed since melting caused the strontium and rubidium to separate. Again, the figure is around 4.5 billion years ago. Still another method of dating is based upon the breakdown of a potassium isotope into argon. The highest figure obtained in this method is 4.3 billion years. Not all of the results agree, however; it is entirely reasonable for one to conclude that meteorites were formed some 4.5 billion years ago. It would seem that they must have formed at the same time that the solar system evolved.

The End of the Earth

You and I have little to worry about, for it appears that life on the earth will not terminate for at least 10 billion years, and it may persist for 100 billion years. If the earth were alone and not affected by the sun, the planet would probably go on and on forever. However, judging by our limited knowledge, we anticipate that the sun will change considerably in the future, and any change in the sun will affect the earth.

One theory holds that the sun will begin to expand within the next few billion years—it will grow bigger and bigger and it will become redder and redder. The sun may become so large that the earth will be inside the solar atmosphere. Mercury, Venus, and earth will change into vapors. Before that time, people may have colonized the outer planets of the solar system, for those planets will have changed. Saturn will be as intensely lighted by the sun as earth is now. Observers on Saturn might live a good life for a few billion years, but then the sun will cool and contract. The rapidly dimming star will become a white dwarf. There will be no one anywhere in the solar system to see events as they transpire. Because of the super-low temperature, all gases will become liquids, and all liquids will become solids. The sun will be one ten-thousandth as bright as it is today and so small that it would appear as a pinpoint. But even though our solar system, or what is left of it, will be cold and forbidding, the sun will still be the center around which the planets move, for its mass and gravitational force will not have decreased very much.

We know enough about the evolution of stars to believe quite strongly that the destiny of the sun, and the earth, will be about as described above. However, there are those who believe the earth will not be vaporized. It will be melted at the surface perhaps, but not destroyed completely. Then, they believe, when the sun cools, another atmosphere will form on the earth and great oceans will evolve. But not for long. As cooling of the sun continues, the atmosphere will become liquid air covering the ice of the oceans to a depth of thirty feet or more.

No matter which alternative occurs, life as we know it will disappear from the earth and from the entire solar system. The planets will become cold, dead, inert, and dark worlds that century after century relentlessly pursue their lonely journeys around a sun that has itself become small and dim, no longer recognizable as the provider of energy, the dominant force of the solar system.

Such possibilities are far removed from our lives. This planet of ours is going to be around for a long, long time. It is going to continue to rotate, revolve, and move in a multitude of other ways, just as it has been moving down through the centuries. In the next chapter we will take a look at the various motions of the earth, and the ways in which these motions affect us.

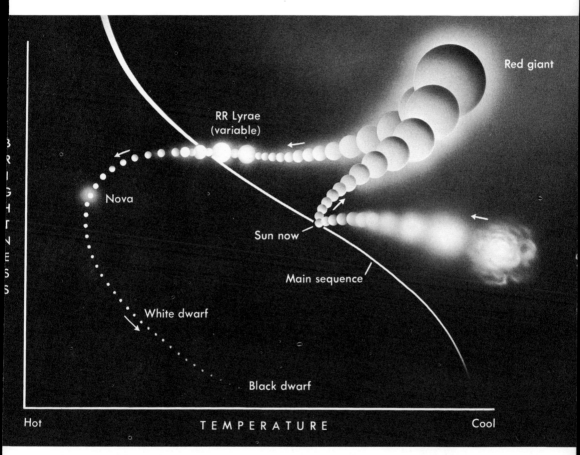

Above, possible evolution of the sun, a star midway on the main sequence of stars.

Below, earth may eventually be surrounded by hot solar atmosphere.

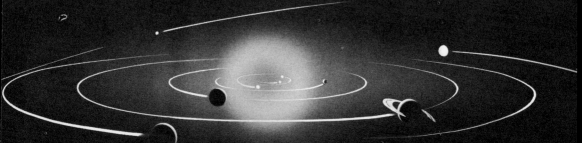

3

MOTIONS OF THE EARTH AND THEIR EFFECTS

LOOKING INTO the daytime sky, the casual sky watcher, and the skilled observer as well, sees the sun rise in the east, move across the sky, and disappear in the west. When one's attention is focused on the night sky, he sees the moon rise, move across the sky, and set in the same fashion as the sun. And so it is with the stars. They seem to make a smooth nightly journey from the eastern to the western horizon. Such observations have been made since man first gazed into the sky. When men wondered about the reasons for such movements, their explanations led inevitably to the conclusion that the earth was motionless; that the earth was a vast, stationary body contained within moving spheres, one each for the sun, moon, planets, and stars. Such ideas were finally incorporated into a philosophy of the universe by Ptolemy, the Greek astronomer who lived in the second century A.D. His theory of the nature of the world influenced the thinking of intelligent men for nearly two thousand years. As late as the seventeenth century in advanced European countries, and well into the eighteenth century in parts of the world that were slower to achieve learning, men were convinced that the earth stood still in space and that the sun, moon, and stars revolved around the planet.

Casual observation confirms the belief that earth stands still and that the objects in the sky are in motion. Look at the sky carefully some night, forget what you know to be true about the nature of the world and base your decisions upon what you can observe and no other factors. You will reach the same conclusions that people did centuries ago; the sun, moon, and stars move around a stationary earth.

But, we have learned that conclusions based upon observations alone are often not valid. We know that the earth does not stand still. Ever since we can remember we have known that the earth rotates, spins on its axis. And we know that the earth revolves around the sun once while it rotates some 365 times. But we know these things not because we found out through our own investigations but only because someone told us or we read about it sometime or other.

Such knowledge is not new. Centuries ago there were curious, questioning men who would not accept what their eyes told them, and who sought correct explanations. In each century holes were made in the wall of ignorance by those who believed that the earth rotated and moved through space. In the fourth century B.C. Herakleides of Pontus taught that the earth turned on its axis. But he was far ahead of his time. His theory denied what people could see with their own eyes. Besides, Herakleides had no way of proving his belief and so it received little more than ridicule.

There were others who believed that the earth moved through space and in a path around the sun. But none of these men received acclaim. People wanted to believe what they saw—the sky moved, and so did everything in the sky. Everything moved around the earth. This is what Hipparchus taught, and Ptolemy, and other early Greek astronomers.

The Polish astronomer Nicolaus Copernicus (1473–1543) could not accept such a model. He believed that the earth and the other planets moved around the sun. Observations on their movements could be explained by such a belief, but he had no proof to back up his ideas.

Now we can prove that the earth revolves and rotates. There are proofs that are positive and rather simple once you understand the principles involved and the procedures that are followed.

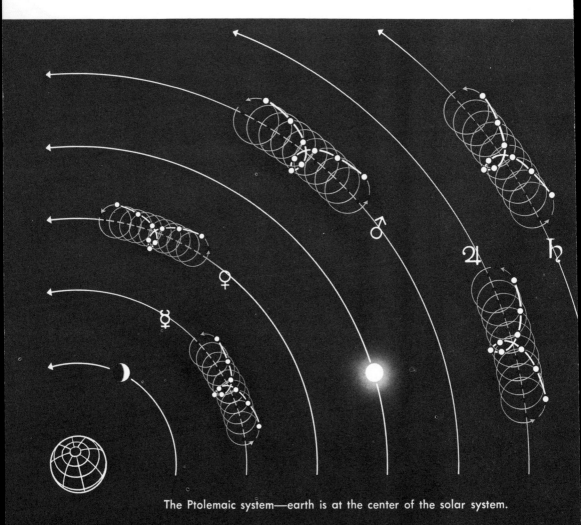

The Ptolemaic system—earth is at the center of the solar system.

Rotation

In the early part of the seventeenth century, telescopes became available and observers were able to see features on the sun, moon, and some planets. They could and did establish that the sun, moon, and planets were rotating. This being so, it was logical to assume that the earth was also rotating. But assumptions are not proofs. Positive proof that the earth was spinning waited upon the experiments of Jean Bernard Leon Foucault (1819–1868), a famous French physicist.

Being a physicist, Foucault knew the basic property of a pendulum—that it swings back and forth in a straight line, or in the same plane. For example, suspend a weight at the end of a length of thread. Set the weight to swinging north to south. While holding the swinging weight, make one complete turn around it, being sure that the pendulum hits nothing. As you turn about, the plane of vibration (motion) of the pendulum remains in a north-south direction. There may be a tendency for the plane of the pendulum to follow you around. This is due to twisting of the thread. If the thread were mounted in a friction-free bearing, the pendulum would continue vibrating in exactly the same plane.

Foucault applied this property of a pendulum to a study of earth's rotation. In 1851 he carried out an experiment in the cellar of his house in Paris. Details of the procedure he followed are not clear. It's hard to imagine how the experiment could have been conducted in a cellar where the wire would have to be short. Perhaps he suspended the weight from a wire that passed through every floor of the house to a bearing fastened to the ceiling of the attic. Maybe that is what he did, but no matter how he devised the experiment, the results he obtained were conclusive—the pendulum could be used to prove that the earth rotates on its axis. Reports are not clear about the identity of the people who witnessed this experiment in the cellar, but we do know that they were impressed. They convinced Foucault he should perform the experiment in a public place so all could see it. The next year, the experiment was conducted again. This time Foucault hung a bronze ball weighing fifty-six pounds from the ceiling of the Pantheon, a high-domed building in Paris. The ball, about a foot in diameter, was at the end of a wire two hundred feet long. A fine needle extended a few inches beyond the ball. This needle was just long enough so as it swung back and forth it scraped through a circle of sand laid on a flat table top. To start the experiment the ball was drawn to one side and held by a piece of string. After several hours to permit all parts of the apparatus to come to rest, the string was burned. The weight was free to swing back and forth at the end of the long wire. Because no other motions were present in the system and because friction had been reduced to the lowest possible amount, the ball swung back and forth, back and forth, always swinging in a plane that passed through the center of the earth.

However, after the first swing the needle at the bottom of the ball cut a new furrow in the sand, a bit to the right of the first furrow. As each swing was completed, the needle cut a new path.

The upper end of the wire from which the weight was suspended was mounted in a bearing having very little friction. Therefore, the pendulum continued to move back and forth in the same plane in which the weight was originally swinging. The floor and ceiling of the Pantheon were turning. The entire building was turning about the pendulum because the building was fastened to the earth and the earth was turning on its axis. After timing the drift to the right, it became quite apparent that the original furrow would be brought under the swinging needle after about thirty-two hours had gone by.

If the experiment were conducted at the North Pole, the weight

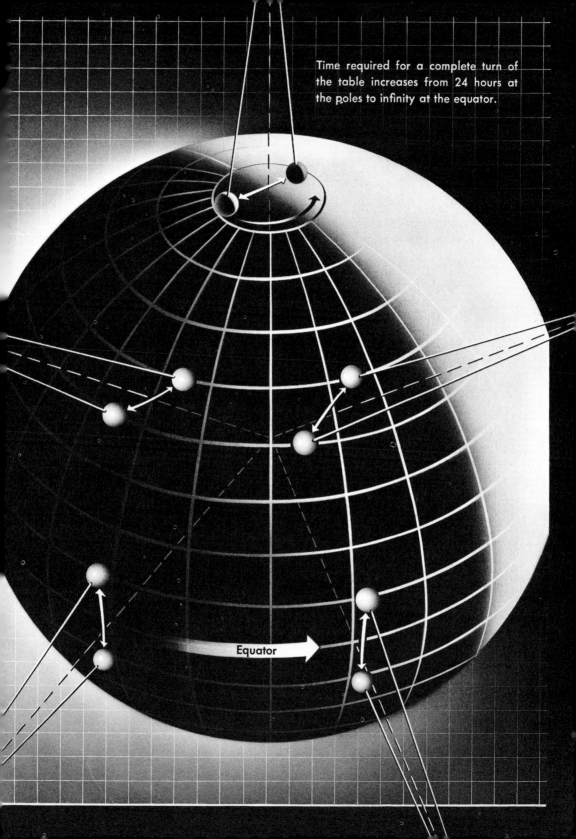

Time required for a complete turn of the table increases from 24 hours at the poles to infinity at the equator.

Equator

would appear to make a complete turn in a clockwise direction in twenty-four hours. If the experiment were conducted at the equator there would be no shift at all, no matter how long the time interval. The time required for the sand table to complete a rotation increases as one moves from the pole, where it is twenty-four hours, to the equator, where the time required for the table to complete a turn is infinite. At any latitude between the equator and the pole, the time required for the weight to move through the original furrow in the sand will be somewhat longer than twenty-four hours. This is because in the northern hemisphere the northern edge of anything, a room or building, is closer to the axis of the earth than the southern edge. The southern edge must therefore move faster than the northern, since both edges must complete a turn in the same period of time. You may understand this condition better if you think of a wheel. All parts of a wheel, the hub which is close to the axis of rotation as well as the rim, must complete a rotation in the same length of time. Since the rim must travel much farther than the hub, the rim must move faster. During a rotation the edge of anything on the earth (the edge toward the equator) must travel farther than the northern edge (the edge toward the pole), therefore it must move faster.

You can see how this works in another way. Look carefully at a globe of the earth, noting particularly the meridians of longitude. Near the equator the meridians are practically parallel. The meridians do not converge at all. At the equator the Foucault pendulum would move parallel to the meridians; there would be no Foucault effect. At the poles the pendulum might be started swinging parallel to a given meridian. But at the poles the meridians converge, so the angle between the pendulum swing and a meridian is maximum, and the Foucault effect is greatest; a cycle is completed in 24 hours.

At any latitude between the equator and a pole, the angle of convergence of the meridians is related to the latitude as shown on page 59—the greater the latitude the greater the angle. The angle is related to the Foucault pendulum time-rate of rotation.

The amount that the pendulum changes from the original plane can be found by multiplying 15° by the sine of the latitude. At New York City, this works out to close to 10° per hour—or 36 hours to complete the circle of 360°.

The sines of the latitudes of different locations in the United States and the amount of hourly deviations are given in the following table:

Location	Latitude	Sine of Latitude	Deviation (degrees per hour)
Florida Keys	25°	.423	6.43
Houston, Texas	30°	.500	7.50
Los Angeles, Calif.	34°	.559	8.38
Decatur, Ill.	40°	.643	9.64
Boston, Mass.	42°	.669	10.03
Bangor, Maine	45°	.707	10.60
Seattle, Wash.	48°	.743	11.14

Except for following changes in the direction of the support, which is vertical from the center of the earth, the pendulum is free to move. Therefore, the pendulum seems to deviate, because of the turning of the earth, and in the direction opposite from the motion of the earth. The earth spins counterclockwise (as viewed from above the North Pole) so the pendulum appears to deviate clockwise.

The Foucault pendulum is the classic experiment for proving that the earth rotates. However, there are other procedures that enable one to reach the same conclusion. One of these makes use of the Doppler shift. An Austrian physicist, Christian Johann Doppler (1803–1835), reasoned that if a light source were moving toward an observer, the light should become bluer. If the source were moving away, then the light should become redder. This idea was later confirmed and explained more fully by a French physicist, Armand Hippolyte Louis Fizeau (1819–1896). This shift toward the blue or the red is often referred to as the Doppler-Fizeau effect.

Astronomers make wide use of the principle because the changes of white light to blue as a light source approaches or from white to red as it recedes are reliable indicators of velocity. To investigate earth's rotation, the following experiment has been suggested. However, there are many factors that make its success highly unlikely.

An artificial satellite carrying a strong light is placed in a non-synchronous orbit. From two locations on the earth—one turning toward the satellite and the other turning away, careful analyses of the light and motions of the satellite would be made. After corrections were computed for the motion of the satellite, the reading at the location moving toward the satellite should show a blue shift, while the reading at the other location should show a change toward red. The amount of shift would indicate earth's rotation and the velocity of rotation. Because radio waves show a Doppler shift just as light waves do, the technique can be followed using radio waves instead of light waves. Indeed, the experiment has been performed many times, and the effect must be considered in solving problems of outer space communications. Results obtained by such procedures would be reliable if the earth were a perfect sphere. Since the earth is far from a perfect sphere, results of studies of earth's rotation made in this manner must be adjusted.

The rotation of the earth produces many effects. For example, rotation affects the directions that winds blow and that ocean currents flow. If the earth were motionless in space, prevailing winds and ocean currents would flow in directions at right angles to the equator. Actually the winds and currents move in quite different ways. They veer to the right in the northern hemisphere and to the left south of the equator. An illustration using bullets fired from hypothetical rifles mounted on the earth may help you to see why.

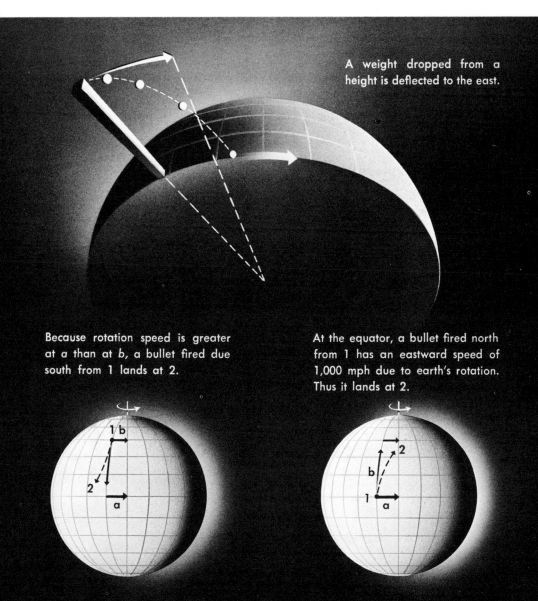

A weight dropped from a height is deflected to the east.

Because rotation speed is greater at *a* than at *b*, a bullet fired due south from 1 lands at 2.

At the equator, a bullet fired north from 1 has an eastward speed of 1,000 mph due to earth's rotation. Thus it lands at 2.

Suppose a rifle at the equator were fired due north. The rifle and the bullet are carried eastward at one thousand miles an hour, the speed of earth's rotation at the equator. The bullet is flying northward from a place moving one thousand miles an hour toward a region that is moving at a slower speed. In effect it speeds ahead of the target toward which it is heading. Therefore, the bullet will land at a location to the right, or east, of the north-south line.

If the rifle is in the far north and pointing southward, the bullet also arrives at a point to the right of a north-south line. In this case the rifle is being carried eastward more slowly than a place farther south. Therefore, during the flight of the bullet, the aiming point is going to move farther eastward than the actual landing point. The bullet will appear to fall behind its target; it will veer to the right, or west.

The effect of earth's rotation on the prevailing winds of the earth is shown in a highly stylized way on the next page. Notice that the arrows veer to the right in every case north of the equator, and to the left in the southern hemisphere. To understand the directions referred to, imagine yourself at the tail of the arrow looking toward the head.

If you could drop a ball from a high tower, as shown on page 59, and if you could determine precisely the point of release and the point of impact, you could see another effect of the rotation of the earth. The ball at the top of the tower is farther from the center of the earth than is earth's surface, therefore, the ball has greater velocity. Recall the wheel analogy referred to earlier. When the ball is dropped it is moving faster eastward than is earth's surface. Therefore, the ball will land a bit farther to the east than it would if the earth were not rotating.

Rotation of the earth on its axis produces the succession of day and night. Because the earth is spherical, or nearly so, one

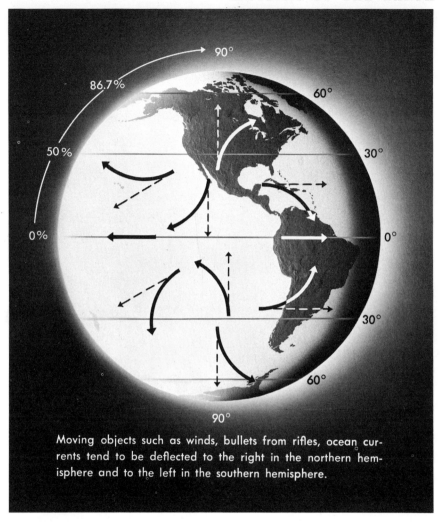

Moving objects such as winds, bullets from rifles, ocean currents tend to be deflected to the right in the northern hemisphere and to the left in the southern hemisphere.

half of the globe is always illuminated by the sun, the other half is in darkness. But the location of the line separating the lighted half from the darkened half changes as the year goes by because of the tilt of earth's axis. The area in space enclosed within earth's orbit might be considered as a flat surface, or plane. The axis of the earth is tilted 23½° from a vertical to the plane of that surface.

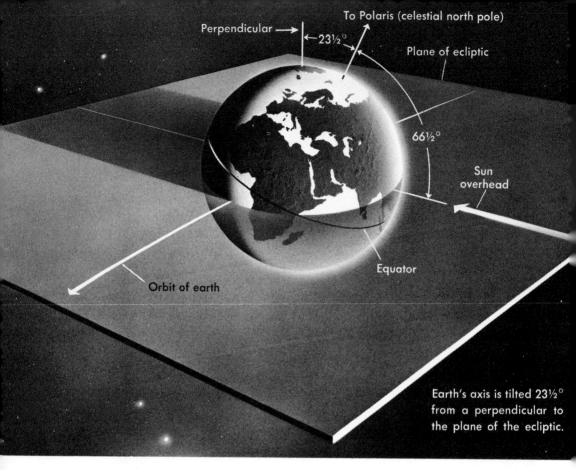

Perpendicular → |← 23½°

To Polaris (celestial north pole)

Plane of ecliptic

66½°

Sun overhead

Equator

Orbit of earth

Earth's axis is tilted 23½° from a perpendicular to the plane of the ecliptic.

Because the tilt remains constant throughout the year, the total number of hours of daylight and darkness that a place on the earth experiences varies from week to week and from month to month. In the tropical regions annual variations in day and night are not large. In the middle latitudes the length of day ranges from about eight hours in winter to almost sixteen hours in summer.

If the axis were vertical to the plane of earth's orbit, the number of hours of day and night at a given location would remain the same year in and year out. If the axis were tilted at an angle of only 2°–3° to the plane of the orbit days and nights would be several months long. This is the case with Uranus, which is tilted

8° to the plane it scribes out in space in its sun-circling journey
of 84 earth years.

Because rotation of the earth is an event that occurs regularly,
it provides us with a basic unit of time. We say quite glibly that
the earth takes 24 hours to make one rotation. The arrangement
is one of convenience, for actually a rotation is completed in less
than 24 hours. To determine when a rotation begins and ends, a
reference point outside the earth such as a star is used. If you
sight a star that is directly overhead or which is on your meridian
(the imaginary line in the sky that extends from pole to pole and
which passes through your zenith) the earth will make one complete turn on its axis before the star will reappear at the same

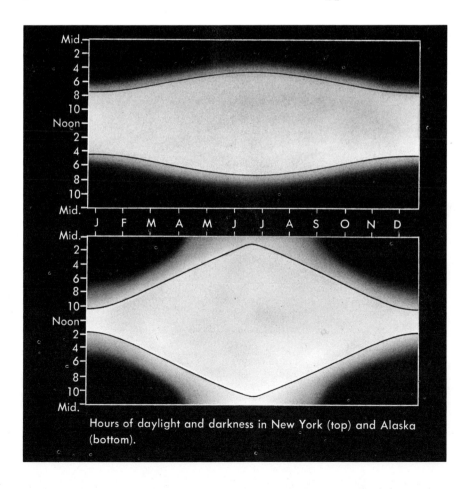

Hours of daylight and darkness in New York (top) and Alaska
(bottom).

location. This interval is called a sidereal day from the Latin word *sidus*, which means "constellation" or "star." The length of the sidereal day is 23 hours 56 minutes 4.090 seconds of mean solar time—or time as measured by a clock. It is the length of time required for the earth to rotate through 360°.

You would find it quite awkward if your watch kept sidereal time. For one thing, "noontime" would occur when the star was on your meridian. This could be anytime during the day or night according to clock time.

Adjustment to such an arrangement would be difficult, so some reference point other than a star is needed for measuring the time required for earth to complete a rotation. The sun is convenient, for by using it we have noon when the sun is at its greatest elevation above the horizon—a situation to which men's affairs have become adjusted. But this arrangement poses its own difficulties, because while the earth rotates, it also revolves around the sun. The effect is that the sun appears to move eastward among the stars, about one degree in a day. Suppose a measurement is started at noon on a given day. By noon of the next day the sun will have changed its position in the sky. Another way of saying this would be that a given location on the earth has to

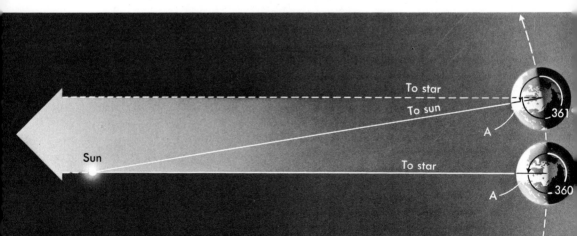

A sidereal day (the time required for point A to turn around once and realign with a star) is about 23 hours 56 minutes. A solar day (the time required for point A to realign with the sun) is about 24 hours.

"catch up" with the sun. To do this, the earth must turn through more than 360°. The time that is required for the earth to catch up with the sun is just about four minutes. Therefore, the day reckoned by the sun is four minutes longer than a sidereal day.

The time kept by our watches and clocks, and time that is used in the affairs of men, is neither sidereal nor solar. The sidereal day cannot be used at all, for reasons mentioned earlier. The solar day—or time reckoned by a sundial—cannot be used because sometimes the sun arrives late at the meridian, at other times it is early. There are two reasons for the variations.

The earth's orbit is an ellipse; therefore the motion of the earth in its orbit is not always the same. Around January 2 the earth moves more rapidly than usual, and around July 2 the motion is slower than usual. This means that the sun as seen from the earth moves unevenly along its path (the ecliptic) through the sky. When the sun is moving slowly, the sun could be at the meridian some seven or eight minutes after clock noon or when moving fast the same interval before clock noon, depending upon the time of the year.

The second reason for the variations in the sun's motions is the fact that clock time is reckoned from a mean sun—an artificial sun if you will—one that moves evenly and smoothly along the equator of the sky. The sun, on the other hand, moves along the ecliptic, and the two lines do not coincide. Suppose, as in the drawing on page 66, earth is at the center and we show the celestial equator and the ecliptic. Make a mark (1) on the ecliptic, halfway between the position the sun occupies on the first day of spring (the spring equinox) and the position the sun occupies on the first day of summer (the summer solstice). Also, put on the equator a mark (2) 45° from the equinox. Obviously, the two points do not coincide. Point 1 is west of point 2 and so will appear first in the sky as the earth rotates. The variation between

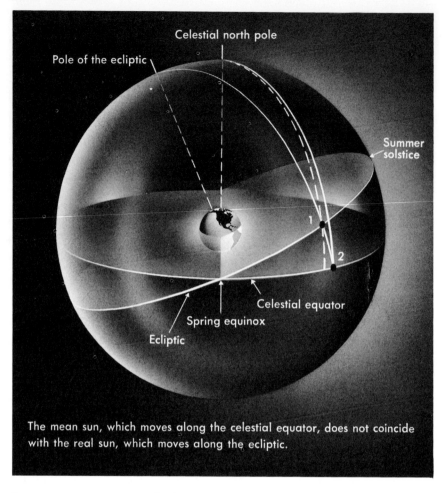

Pole of the ecliptic

Celestial north pole

Summer
solstice

Celestial equator

Spring equinox

Ecliptic

The mean sun, which moves along the celestial equator, does not coincide
with the real sun, which moves along the ecliptic.

the apparent sun and the mean sun produced by this effect
amounts to ten minutes fast or slow.

The two causes of variations in the apparent solar day (time
reckoned by a sundial) and the mean solar day (time kept by
a watch) can be charted to produce what is called the equation
of time. The dotted line shows effects caused by the fact that the
ecliptic and the equator do not coincide, and the dashed line
shows effects caused by the fact that the apparent motion of the

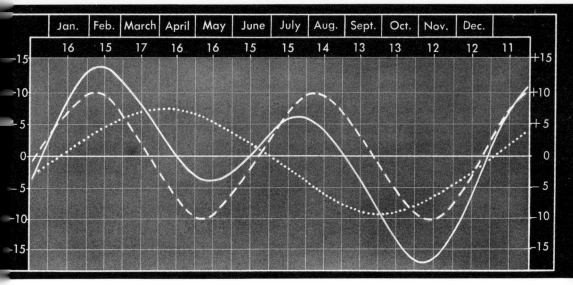

Jan.	Feb.	March	April	May	June	July	Aug.	Sept.	Oct.	Nov.	Dec.
16	15	17	16	16	15	15	14	13	13	12	12	11

The equation of time (solid line) results from the variable motion of the sun along the ecliptic (dashed line) and the divergence of the equator and the ecliptic (dotted line).

sun is not uniform throughout the year. The heavy line represents the total effect of the two causes. To adjust a sundial reading to clock time add minutes to the sundial figure when the heavy line is above the zero line, subtract minutes when the heavy line is below the zero line.

Aside from the above considerations, which are concerned with conditions outside the earth, the earth itself is a good clock because its sidereal period of rotation remains fairly constant. However, when considered critically, earth's period of rotation is variable. For example, the rotation time of earth is increasing. Tides produced by the moon cause water to rush through long channels and bays which sets up frictional drag. In the course of one hundred years, the drag causes the length of earth's period of rotation to be increased by a bit more than one one-thousandth of a second. In addition to this change, which is cumulative, there are seasonal variations in earth's rotation in the order of two or three hundredths of a second. The effect is for the earth to be slow usually in the spring and fast in the autumn relative to a uniform time. These changes that are related to seasons are probably brought about by shifts in large air masses, by the melting of the polar ice caps, and by variations in the energy of motion of the atmosphere. Measures of such fractional time intervals must be looked upon warily, for the measurement can be no better than the timing device itself. A major problem in obtaining such conclusions is concerned with the development of clocks more reliable than the rotation period of earth itself. Because of their near-perfect performance, quartz crystal and cesium clocks are often used to time astronomical events and those involving man-made satellites and space probes.

Revolution

The most casual skywatcher is aware that the noontime sun appears at different elevations above the horizon as the seasons go by. In the northern hemisphere in springtime, the sun rides higher, reaching the zenith at the Tropic of Cancer on the first day of summer. As the weeks go by after the summer solstice, the noonday sun rides successively lower, reaching the lowest elevation on the first day of winter. As seen from the vicinity of New York at the winter solstice the noonday sun would be only 26 degrees above the horizon. As seen from the Tropic of Capricorn the noontime sun would be directly overhead.

Today we are quite aware of the cause of these changes. But once again, our awareness has not grown from actual observation. Rather it is knowledge that we have been told about or that we have gathered from our own reading. Ptolemy, an early Greek astronomer, explained the changes in the position of the sun by supposing that the earth was standing still in space. He believed that the sun rode along a great spiral having 183 turns (one half of 365). When it was at the top of the spiral, there was summer in the northern hemisphere, and winter came when the sun had reached the bottom of the spiral. During the first half of the year, the sun rode down the spiral; during the second half it retraced the path. This was not such a bad explanation, for it certainly did give reasons, however wrong they were, for the gross observations of the northward and southward journeys of the sun.

But there was another motion to be explained. As the year went by, the sun appeared to move eastward among the stars. This is not apparent when one observes the sun directly, for the stars around it that furnish a background against which position changes may be noted are not visible in the daytime. But one can see readily that the stars opposite the sun, those rising in the east as the sun disappears below the western horizon, do change from season to season. In winter, the constellation Orion rises as the sun sets, in spring it is Leo, while in summer Scorpius is the constellation that first appears above the eastern horizon, and Pegasus dominates the autumn skies.

These changes in the stars throughout the year can be explained by supposing the earth is stationary, and the sun and stars move around it. However, there are fine measurements and observations that can be explained in only one way—by the revolution of the earth around the sun. One of these observations is the aberration of starlight.

Aberration of Starlight

The word *aberration* comes from a Latin word which means "to stray." In astronomy the word has meaning, for stars are not always precisely where they ought to be; they seem to stray.

Slight changes in the positions of stars; changes related to earth's location in its orbit, were observed and reported in 1725 by the English astronomer James Bradley (1693–1762), although the effect had probably been observed earlier, but without explanation. Bradley was not able to explain his observations either until 1729, when quite by accident he found a reason for the apparent straying of certain stars. He and an associate, Samuel Molyneux, were interested in finding out if stars made apparent shifts in position as the year went by. They constructed a telescope which was permanently directed at or near the zenith. The telescope was built inside a house just outside of London. It was fastened to the chimney to hold it motionless, and extended through the ceiling to the attic. An opening was cut in the roof so the zenith could be viewed. After several months they found that the star nearest the zenith seemed to shift some 40″. You recall that in referring to angular position the degree (0°) is used; the degree is divided into 60 minutes (60′), and the minute is further divided into 60 seconds (60″). Therefore, 40″ is not a large change in position from the layman's standpoint; however, it is considerable from the standpoint of the astronomer. Bradley constructed another, more accurate, telescope to make further observations. In every case Bradley found that there were displacements of the stars, and the displacements were always essentially the same amount—close to 40″.

The explanation for these changes came to Bradley not through careful, systematic procedures, but quite accidentally. While he was sailing on the Thames River, Bradley noticed that the wind vane on the mast shifted as the boat changed course, even though the wind was steady. This suggested to him that starlight was steady just as was the wind, and the displacements he observed were caused by earth's motion, a fact that has since been established.

Let's see how this works out. Suppose we think of starlight as a stream of particles coming to us from a star. If we are moving, then the particles will seem to come from a location different from their actual source. It is somewhat the same as a man walking through a rainstorm, the drops falling from directly overhead.

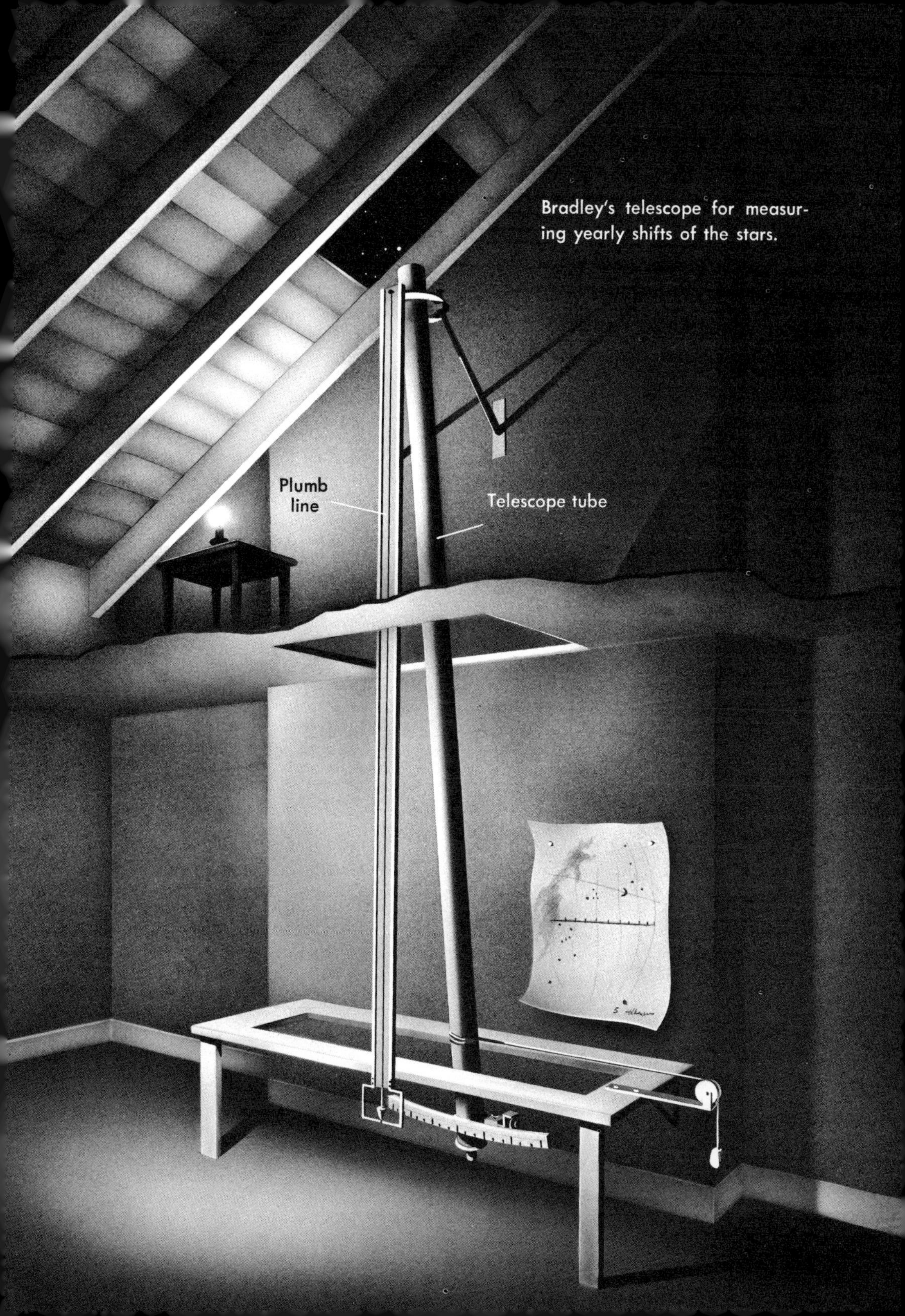

Bradley's telescope for measuring yearly shifts of the stars.

Plumb line

Telescope tube

If the man stands still, he can protect himself by holding an umbrella directly overhead. If the man walks he must tilt the umbrella in the direction he moves. The faster he walks, the more he must tilt the umbrella to keep dry. The rain seems to be coming from a direction other than overhead.

One way of lining up a star is to point a tube at it. Starlight must go in one end of the tube and out the other if we are to see it. The diagram shows the rays of light coming from a star. Light goes in the upper end of the tube and it goes out the lower end. Let's think of a single "particle" of light. It enters the top of the tube. While the light is traveling through the tube, the entire tube is being carried from left to right by earth's motion around the sun. The tube must be slanted as shown if the bottom of the tube and the light are to arrive at the same place at the same time.

It makes no difference if the tube is long or short. Suppose the tube were 186,000 miles long. Light would then take one second to travel from the top to the bottom. During that second the earth would travel about 18.5 miles in its orbit. The tube would have to be slanted so that the bottom of the tube was 18.5 miles behind the top of the tube. In astronomy, telescopes must be slanted so the base trails the top of the tube. In order for a star to be seen,

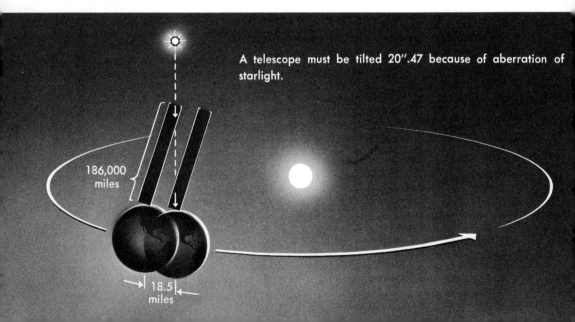

A telescope must be tilted 20".47 because of aberration of starlight.

186,000 miles

18.5 miles

the tube must be tilted forward 20.47". This is the constant of aberration. In observing planets as well as stars aberration must be considered.

The effect of aberration upon the apparent positions of the stars is shown in the diagram on page 74, where we see earth in different positions in its orbit around the sun. Star *A* is at the pole of the ecliptic (this is a point 90° from the ecliptic), while star *B* is on the ecliptic itself. When the earth is at position 1, star *A* is displaced to the left, toward us when at 2, to the right when at position 3 and away from us at 4. The effect is for star *A* to appear to describe a circle having a diameter of 41". Because earth is moving toward star *B* in position 1 and away from the star in position 2, no aberration is noted. However, at 2 and 4 apparent shifts are seen. These amount to an annual apparent change of 41".

Stars along the ecliptic move back and forth through 41", while those at locations between the ecliptic and the pole appear to scribe out complete ellipses. The major axis of such ellipses is always 41", as shown in the illustration.

The velocity with which the earth moves in its orbit, and the distance from the earth to the sun, can be computed by using the constant of aberration. The relationship is expressed in the following equation:

$$\text{tangent } a = \frac{u}{v}, \text{ or}$$

$$\frac{\text{tangent of angle}}{\text{of aberration}} = \frac{\text{velocity of earth}}{\text{velocity of light}} \text{ or}$$

$$\text{tangent } 20''47 = \frac{x}{186{,}273\,(299{,}766 \text{ km/sec.})}$$

$$x = 299{,}776 \text{ tangent } 20''47$$
$$x = 29.75 \text{ km/sec } (18.49 \text{ mi/sec})$$

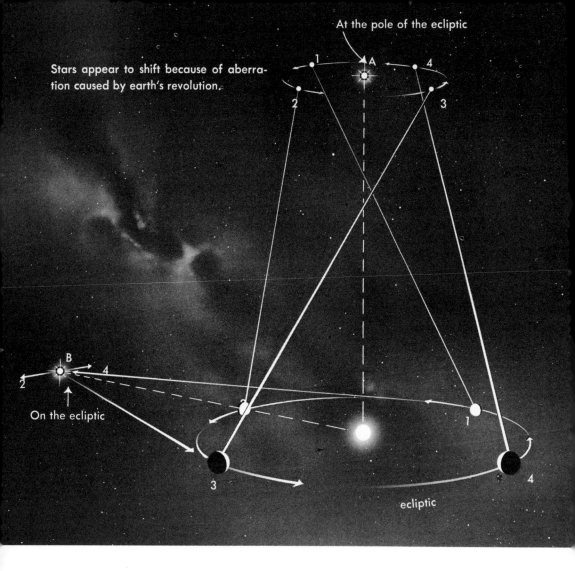

At the pole of the ecliptic

Stars appear to shift because of aberration caused by earth's revolution.

On the ecliptic

ecliptic

We know that a sidereal year is the time required for the earth to revolve through 360°. If we determine the number of seconds there are in a sidereal year and then multiply this by 18.49 we will have the circumference of earth's orbit. The length of the sidereal year is 31,558,149.5 seconds. When this is worked out, the circumference of the earth's orbit (assuming it to be circular, which it very nearly is) is found to be 583,510,184.25 miles.

The circumference of a circle is related to the radius as follows:

$$2\pi R = \text{circumference}$$
$$R = \frac{\text{circumference}}{2\pi}$$
$$R = \frac{583,510,184}{2 \times 3.1416}$$

When this relationship is worked out the radius of earth's orbit (distance to the sun) is found to be very nearly 92,900,000 miles. This figure agrees closely with the measurements obtained in other ways, such as by accurate determination of the period of Eros, a short-period asteroid, and by careful measurement of the parallax of the sun.

Parallactic Displacement

The parallactic displacement (apparent shifting) of nearby stars is another observation that can be explained only by the earth's revolution around the sun.

In the third century B.C. Aristarchus, a Greek scholar, believed that the earth traveled through space. Aristotle, who lived at the same time, contended that the earth was fixed and immovable. After all, said Aristotle, if earth truly traveled through space we should be carried into different regions of the stars at different times of the year. This would change the appearance of the constellations. Since the arrangement of stars in constellations did not change, Aristotle concluded that the earth did not travel as Aristarchus contended.

Aristotle was right in saying that earth's revolution should cause a shifting of the stars, for the stars do indeed shift. However, the changes are so slight that a person is not aware of them. Delicate instruments are required to detect them.

Suppose a star were nearby, as in the diagram on pages 76-77,

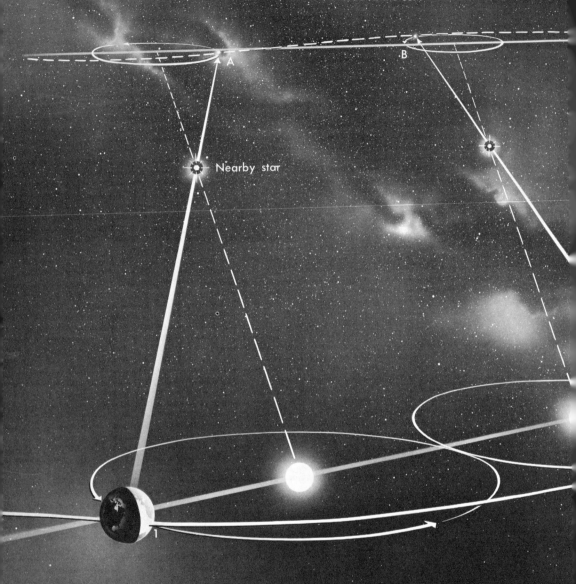

Parallax results from earth's revolution around the sun.

B

A

Nearby star

Viewed from a star, the sun in one year moves along a straight line, and the earth is seen at various positions which produce the heavy line when joined together. The apparent orbit of the earth is indicated (bottom). Reversing directions, seen from the sun a nearby star appears to move along the solid line. When viewed from the earth, the star appears to move along the dashed line (upper part).

Earth and sun move through space.

and that the other stars were much farther away. If the earth were fixed, the star would always appear in the same location among the distant stars. If the earth moves in an orbit, then the star would appear at *A* when the earth is at position 1, and it would appear to be at *B* when earth is at position 2. This is precisely what happens. The fact is that nearby stars appear to scribe out ellipses in space—small counterparts of the shape of earth's orbit as it revolves around the sun. An observer located at the position of the sun would see the star move across the sky along the solid line in the upper part of the illustration on pages 76-77. From earth the star would seem to move in ellipses as shown. The solid line is the proper motion of the star. The dashed line is the annual parallax of the star.

Eclipsing of Jovian Satellites

In 1675 Olaus Roemer, a Danish physicist, discovered that time is required for light to travel from one place to another. Previous to this discovery people believed that light occurred instantaneously, for as soon as a torch was lighted the entire area around it was also lighted. Light seemed to be everywhere at once. Roemer made his discovery by making a careful study of the time that elapsed between eclipses of four of Jupiter's satellites—those that had been discovered by Galileo some sixty-five years earlier. Roemer found that the eclipses occurred at intervals so regular that he could predict the events. He could do this so precisely that it was possible to prepare a timetable. At first the timetable worked out well—the eclipses occurred at the predicted moment. But after a while the observed times of the eclipses did not agree with the timetable. The eclipses occurred later and later, and then after a time the delay became smaller and smaller. Suppose observations of the eclipses were first made while earth was at the part of its orbit nearest Jupiter. Roemer found that the intervals between eclipses increased during the succeeding months until earth had reached the location in its orbit most distant from Jupiter. Then, as the earth moved toward the planet, the error in the predicted time grew steadily less. When the earth had reached the original position, the eclipses were again on time. Roemer concluded correctly that the alternate delay and speed-up of the eclipses was due to the changing time required for light

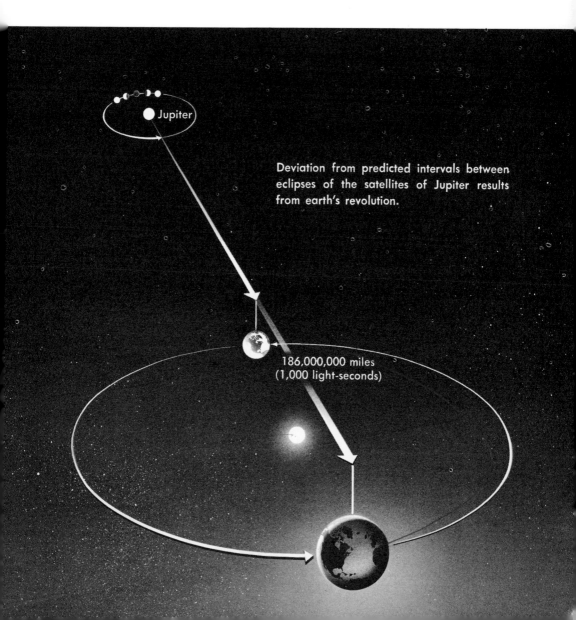

Jupiter

Deviation from predicted intervals between eclipses of the satellites of Jupiter results from earth's revolution.

186,000,000 miles
(1,000 light-seconds)

to travel from the satellites to the earth. But for our purposes, the investigation provides still another proof that the earth is moving in a great orbit around the sun. However, this explanation is not foolproof, for one must remember that the same time differences would be apparent if the earth were stationary and Jupiter were approaching and receding from us. Therefore, considered alone, the changes do not necessarily result from earth's motion around the sun, although they certainly support the contention, for we cannot conceive of a planet alternately approaching and receding from the earth in the implied manner and time interval.

Eclipsing Stars

An effect similar to that produced when the satellites of Jupiter are seen from different positions in the orbit of the earth is noted when observations are made of certain eclipsing binary stars. These are two-star systems in which two stars go around each other and the plane of revolution is in our line of sight.

When the eclipsing of these stars occurs we find that while the earth is receding from the stars the time of occurrence lags behind that which has been predicted. When the earth is approaching the star system, the eclipsing occurs before the time determined by prediction. It is quite ridiculous to suppose that each of the star systems is alternately moving toward the earth and then receding, completing the cycle in just one year. Therefore, this time lag and speed-up is accepted as evidence supporting the contention that the earth moves in an orbit.

Another observation of stars affords further indications of effects produced by the revolution of the earth around the sun.

Yearly Variations in Radial Velocities

The radial velocity of a star is the rate at which the distance between the star and earth changes. If the distance is decreasing, the star has negative radial velocity; if increasing, the star has positive radial velocity. Stars are so far away that their motions across the sky are very small. However, motions of the stars or of objects moving toward the stars can be measured by observing shift of spectral lines. Radial velocities can be determined to within a small fraction of one mile per second by careful analysis of this shift—the Doppler-Fizeau effect.

From the drawing on page 76 it is apparent that if the earth is revolving around the sun, it will, at a given time of the year, be moving toward a certain star on the ecliptic. Six months later the earth will be moving away from the same star. For example, in January orbital motion will carry the earth toward the stars in Virgo and away from those in Aries. In July, the situation is reversed.

Stars do have motions of their own. However, repeated observations of radial velocities of stars reveals that in January the radial velocities of all the stars in Virgo will be about thirty kilometers per second greater and in Aries thirty kilometers per second less than in April and October when the earth is moving at right angles to the stars. Observations of stars in other parts of the zodiac give similar results. The observations support the idea that the earth travels around the sun in a nearly circular path with a velocity of about thirty kilometers (18 miles) a second; approximately one ten-thousandth of the velocity of light.

These observations and explanations are strongly supported by inferences and assumptions. We know that the satellites of the planets go around their mother planets, for we can observe the motions. Likewise, we know that Venus travels in a great orbit for we can see the phasing of the planet—a phenomenon that can be explained only because we see the planet in various positions as it goes around the sun. Saturn's rings are seen in different perspectives—sometimes edge on, sometimes almost full view—because the tilt of the rings is fixed and because the planet travels around the sun. Careful and prolonged observation of almost any celestial object reveals that the object travels in a great orbit. Therefore it is logical to assume that earth must move in a similar fashion.

Shape of Earth's Orbit

Hipparchus, a Greek scholar, noticed that the sun required 186 days to move from the vernal equinox to the autumnal equinox and only 179 days to return. In those days the skies and everything in the sky were believed to move perfectly and around the earth. This meant that the sun had to move in a circle—the perfect geometric form. Also, each object in the sky had to move at a uniform velocity. If the earth were at the center of the circle, then the sun would take the same length of time to travel through any given half of the sky. Observations showed this was not the case. Hipparchus explained the difference by saying that the earth is a bit off-center.

While this explanation was quite satisfactory, it was not correct, for we know that the earth moves around the sun and that its orbit is elliptical, causing the velocity of the earth to vary. This results in variations in the length of the seasons.

Careful measurements made at various times throughout the year of the diameter of the sun enable a model of earth's orbit to be constructed. This procedure works because an object appears larger the closer we are to it.

A model of the shape of earth's orbit can be constructed as follows. A point S is selected to represent the sun, and a line is drawn from S to another point representing the vernal equinox. Additional lines of indefinite length are drawn from S, the angle the line makes with the line first drawn being the longitude of the sun—angle east of the vernal equinox. If lines are drawn at

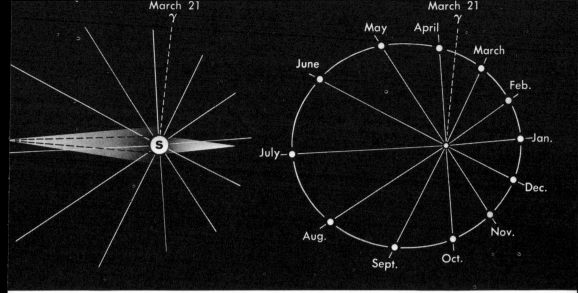

The angles of the shaded cones are equal. The apparent size of the sun at perihelion is represented by the cone at the right; the apparent size of the sun at aphelion is shown by the dashed lines at left.

intervals throughout the year, on the first of each month let us say, then we have a drawing that shows the direction of the earth as seen from the sun on each of those days. In order to construct an orbit, we need to know the relative distances between the sun and earth on each date. On the first of each month a measurement is made of the diameter of the sun. Typical measurements are as follows:

Month	Solar Semi-Diameter in Seconds of Arc
October	960 (10.41)
January	978 (10.20)
April	962 (10.38)
July	945 (10.48)

If we divide these figures into 10,000, a number chosen to give us a manageable measurement, we have values for the length of each line as shown in the parentheses. The first line should be drawn any convenient length determined by the size chosen for the entire drawing.

Each of the lines drawn earlier is cut so the length is proportional to the values in parentheses. When the ends of the lines are connected, we have a model of earth's orbit. One could not discern that the orbit is not circular. However, as can be seen from the drawing, the center of the circle is quite a bit removed from the sun itself. The shape of earth's orbit is found to be an ellipse with the sun at one of the foci. The eccentricity of the ellipse is about one sixtieth.

Since we are discussing ellipses it might be a good idea to digress for a moment or so to study the ellipse itself. By definition, an ellipse is a closed curve in which the sum of the distances from any point to the two foci is constant and equal to the major axis. You can see how this works by constructing an ellipse. Stick two pins into a piece of cardboard. Place a loop of thread loosely over the pins. With the point of a pencil tighten the loop and draw a curve, keeping the loop tight at all times. The sum of the distances from the pins to the pencil is constant, being equal to the length of the entire loop less the distance between the pins.

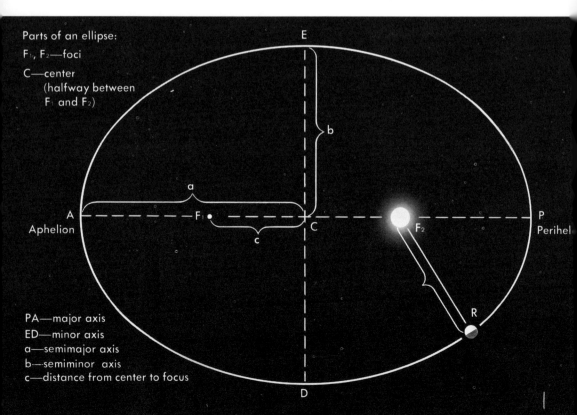

Parts of an ellipse:
F_1, F_2—foci
C—center
(halfway between
F_1 and F_2)

A
Aphelion

E

b

a

c

C

F_2

P
Perihel

R

D

PA—major axis
ED—minor axis
a—semimajor axis
b—semiminor axis
c—distance from center to focus

The various parts of the ellipse are shown in the illustration. The eccentricity (e) of an ellipse is obtained by dividing the distance from the center to a focus (c) by the length of the semi-major axis (a).

$$e \text{ (eccentricity)} = \frac{c}{a}$$

In order for the figure to be an ellipse, the eccentricity must be less than one. Earth's orbit has an eccentricity of one sixtieth, or 0.016.

Earth's orbit is shown with eccentricity greatly exaggerated in the illustration on page 84. The sun is at one of the foci. Perihelion is the point on the orbit where the earth is closest to the sun—it is at one end of the major axis. It is the location from which the sun will appear to be largest. The other end of the major axis is called aphelion—the location where earth is at the greatest distance from the sun and from which the sun appears to be smallest. The earth is at perihelion around January 4, and it is at aphelion on or about July 4.

A line drawn from the earth to the sun—SR for example, is a radius vector. The angle BSR is the planet's anomaly, an angle that obviously is always changing. The mean distance of a planet from the sun is the mean of the perihelion and aphelion distances; it is also the semimajor axis of the ellipse. Another term related to an ellipse is the line of apsides. This is simply the major axis extended indefinitely. It is called the line of apsides because either perihelion or aphelion is often referred to as an apsis.

Because earth's orbit is an ellipse we have an explanation for the fact, as observed by Hipparchus, that 186 days are needed for the sun to travel from the vernal equinox to the autumnal equinox while only 179 days are needed for the return journey. In 1609, the German astronomer-mathematician Johannes Kepler discovered a basic law controlling the revolution of a planet. He

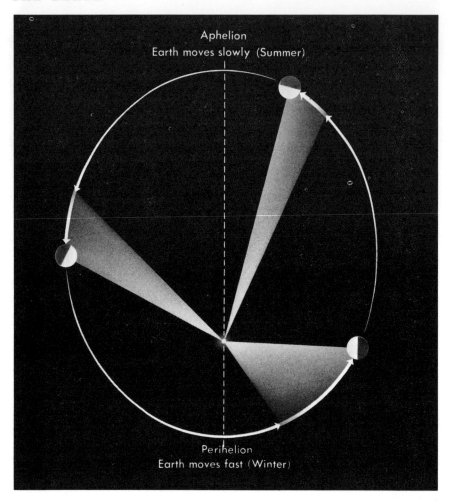

Aphelion
Earth moves slowly (Summer)

Perihelion
Earth moves fast (Winter)

Areas swept out by a radius vector in a given period of time are equal.

found that the area swept out by a radius vector is always the same in any given period of time. Therefore, when earth is close to the sun (perihelion) it moves more rapidly than when it is at aphelion. The mean velocity of earth in its orbit around the sun is 18.5 miles per second (97,680 feet per second)—the velocity at aphelion is 96,100 feet per second, while that at perihelion is 99,300 feet per second.

As earth travels around the sun, the center of the earth does not describe the orbit, but rather the orbit is determined by the center of gravity of the earth-moon system. The earth and moon may be considered a double planetary system that revolves around the sun. You might think of the earth and moon as two bodies that move around a "center of balance," much as two persons balance on a seesaw at the same time that the "center of balance," or barycenter, moves in a smooth ellipse around the sun. Because the earth is much more massive than the moon, the "center of balance" must be closer to the earth than to the moon. Indeed, it is within the earth itself. Both the earth and the moon move around the "center of balance" as they revolve around the sun. The moon moves in a wide swing, the earth moves in a much smaller path.

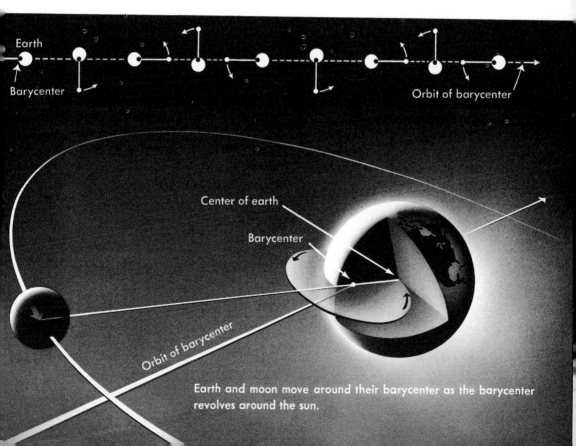

Earth and moon move around their barycenter as the barycenter revolves around the sun.

Sometimes the earth is ahead of its center; sometimes it is behind. The sun is observed against the sky at a point directly opposite earth's location. Therefore, the sun will sometimes appear behind its predicted position, and sometimes it will be ahead. With sensitive instruments, the discrepancies in the sun's positions can be measured. Once they are obtained, mathematicians can determine the location of the barycenter of the earth-moon system. It is 2,903 miles from the center of the earth.

Effects of Earth's Revolution Around the Sun

As mentioned earlier, rotation of the earth is fairly constant and so when the rotation is measured by using some fixed point in the sky it serves as a clock. The succession of day and night is produced by earth's rotation. The succession of seasons is produced by earth's revolution.

The axis of the earth is tilted 23½° from a vertical to the plane of earth's orbit. Throughout the year, the axis remains parallel with any previous position and pointing in the general direction of Polaris—the star is not directly at the location toward which the pole is directed, but is removed by about one degree. When the North Pole is tilted toward the sun, the northern hemisphere enjoys summer. Sunlight falls on the earth beyond the North Pole. Six months later, because earth's axis remains parallel to itself, the South Pole is tilted toward the sun, and sunlight reaches beyond that pole.

At the time of the summer solstice—around June 21—the northern hemisphere receives the greatest amount of energy. At that time the sun is in the sky the greatest number of hours and radiation from the sun is received at the most direct angle. But June is not the hottest time of the year. The temperature continues to rise during July and into August because the region receives more heat than it loses—the earth gets hotter. And the temperature continues to increase until heat loss equals heat intake. This usually occurs in August. In similar fashion, the northern hemisphere is not coldest in December, when the sun has reached its lowest elevation in the sky. The region continues to lose heat until early February when heat loss equals heat gain—after which time there is gradual warming.

Earlier we pointed out that during winter in the northern hemisphere earth is closest to the sun, and during summer it is farthest away. Many people find this hard to believe, thinking that earth temperatures should then be reversed. However, the difference in distance is very little, for the distance of earth from the sun in January is only about 3 percent less than it is in July. However, the fact is that the earth as a whole does receive about 6 percent more heat during the northern winter. Seasons would have greater extremes of temperature in the southern hemisphere than in the northern if the surface covered by land masses were similar. However, the southern hemisphere has great bodies of water which temper the climate—warming the winters and cooling the summers.

One Revolution Equals One Year?

A year is the time required for the earth to make one revolution about the sun. Another way of saying this is that a year is the time interval between two successive appearances of the sun in the same part of the sky. As the earth goes around the sun, the sun appears to move from west to east against the background stars. The location in the sky usually selected as the starting point for measuring this motion is the vernal, or spring, equinox. It is that place where the celestial equator (an extension of earth's equator to the sky) and the ecliptic intersect, and through which the sun passes on the first day of spring. The interval between two appearances of the sun at the vernal equinox is called the tropical year. The word *tropical* as used here has no connection with the tropical zone, but is derived from the Greek word *trope* which means "turning." The length of the tropical year is 365 days, 5 hours, 48 minutes, and 46 seconds—$365^d5^h48^m46^s$, or 365.242 days. The year according to the calendar contains exactly 365 days. Obviously there's a problem here, for if the situation were allowed to continue, the calendar would get out of step with events—after a while the winter solstice would occur in springtime of the year and the timing of events would become most confusing. We attempt to correct this error by introducing an extra day every fourth year.

This day added to February makes our leap year. But adding a whole day does not solve the problem. A whole day is 11 minutes, 14 seconds too much. After one hundred years this would add up to 18 hours, 43 minutes too much. So, every one hundred years we do not have a leap year. But you can readily see that we still have a problem.

In leaving out a whole day we leave out 5 hours, 17 minutes too much. In four hundred years this amounts to more than 21 hours. We solve this problem by putting in an extra day every four hundred years. Obviously every four hundred years we are putting back too much—so much that in 3428 it will amount to a whole day. In that far-off year calendar makers will again have to make adjustments, for the calendar must be kept in step with the seasons.

We reckon time and events by seasons. Since the seasons depend upon the sun's place in the sky, the year in general use is the tropical year—the year of the seasons. However, the year may be measured in other ways. Suppose we were to line up the sun with a distant star. The time that elapsed until the sun lined up with the star again would be a sidereal year. This interval of the sidereal year is $365^d6^h9^m9^s.5$ of mean solar time. It is approximately twenty minutes longer than the tropical year.

The two years—tropical and sidereal—do not agree because of precession of the earth's axis.

Precession and the Tropical Year

Earlier we mentioned that the vernal equinox is a point in the sky where the celestial equator and the ecliptic intersect; it is the place in the sky where the sun is located at the beginning of spring, the moment when, by tradition, the year begins. However, the location of that point is changing continually, moving westward among the stars. The westward drift of the vernal equinox appears to have been discovered by Hipparchus, who lived in the second century B.C., and was first explained by Copernicus as a result of a motion similar to that of a gyroscope. Hipparchus computed, and quite accurately, that in 3000 B.C. the equinox was in the constellation Taurus, perhaps among the oldest of the constellations and certainly the best known by people of ancient days, for it was the constellation where the year started. In the days of Hipparchus, the equinox had moved to the constellation Aries, and now it is in the constellation Pisces. The equinox will continue to move toward the west, reaching the constellation Taurus—the location it held in the earliest days of the zodiac—around the year A.D. 23,000.

This westward migration of the equinoxes is called precession of the equinoxes, or simply precession—from *precede* meaning "to go before." It is a motion of the earth caused by the attraction of the sun and moon, primarily the moon, on the equatorial bulge of the earth.

If the earth were not spinning, there would be no precession. Because it is spinning, the earth behaves like a gyroscope. This means that it moves at right angles to any force that is exerted upon it.

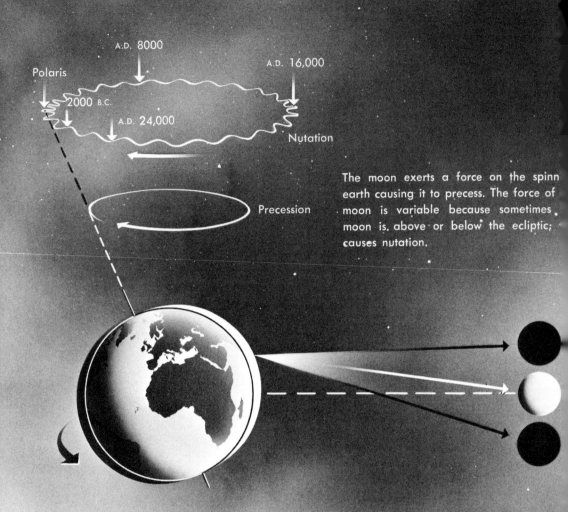

Polaris

A.D. 8000

A.D. 16,000

2000 B.C.

A.D. 24,000

Nutation

Precession

The moon exerts a force on the spinn
earth causing it to precess. The force of
moon is variable because sometimes
moon is above or below the ecliptic;
causes nutation.

Because of precession the location of the vernal equinox shifts westward about
50 seconds of arc a year. In 3000 B.C. it was in Taurus; it is now in Pisces.

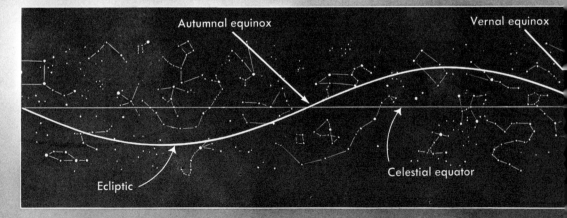

Autumnal equinox

Vernal equinox

Ecliptic

Celestial equator

The equator of the earth, and therefore the equatorial bulge, is tilted 23½° from the plane of the ecliptic. The moon is on the ecliptic, or nearly so. Because of its nearness to the earth, the moon exerts considerably more attraction on the side of earth's bulge toward the moon than the side away from the moon. The effect is to tend to place the axis of rotation at right angles to the ecliptic. Because the earth is spinning, it resists this force, moving at right angles to it. The result is that the axis of the earth moves so as to describe a vast cone—the apex angle of which is 47°—twice 23½°, the angle of earth's axis from the vertical. The motion of the axis is retrograde, which means it is opposite to the direction of earth's rotation. The force exerted by the moon is very small compared with the mass of the earth and its momentum; therefore the earth precesses very slowly.

The inclination of earth's axis will remain at 23½°; however, over a period of time the axis will point to different parts of the sky. Polaris is our pole star at the present time, but it was not always so. In the days of the Egyptians the pole star was Thuban, a bright star in the constellation Draconis, the dragon. You may find Thuban about halfway between Mizar, the star in the middle of the handle of the Big Dipper, and the two stars that make the end of the bowl of the Little Dipper.

Presently the axis points about one degree from Polaris. About six thousand years from now the star Alpha Cephei will be the star nearest to the location in the sky to which the axis will point. In A.D. 14,000 Vega will be the pole star, although it will be quite a bit removed from the pole itself. About A.D. 28,000 Polaris will once again be the pole star. A precession cycle is completed in about twenty-six thousand years.

In addition to changes in the pole star the apparent positions of other stars relative to the horizon change because of precession. For example, in 4000 B.C. the Southern Cross could be seen

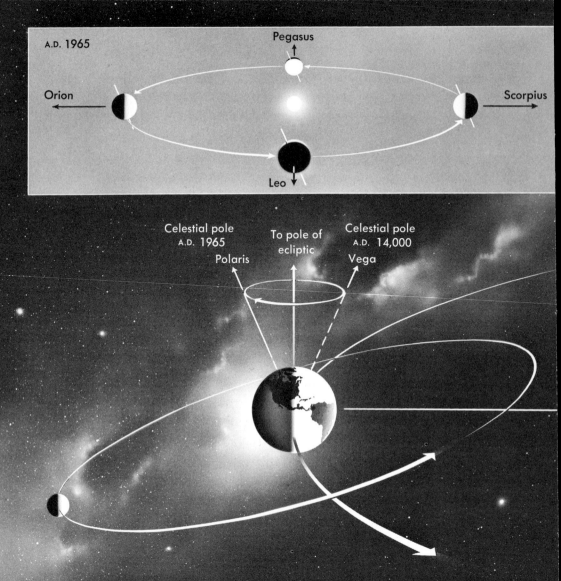

A.D. 1965

Pegasus

Orion

Scorpius

Leo

Celestial pole
A.D. 1965
Polaris

To pole of
ecliptic

Celestial pole
A.D. 14,000
Vega

Precession will eventually cause summer and winter to occur at opposite locations in earth's orbit.

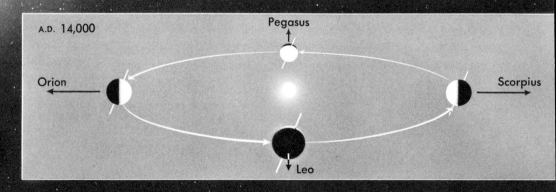

A.D. 14,000

Pegasus

Orion

Scorpius

Leo

from Germany and England. Now, one has to be considerably farther south to see these stars.

As the precession cycle continues, more extreme changes in the stars will occur. Right now Orion is a winter constellation for observers living in the northern hemisphere, and Scorpius is a summer constellation. Around A.D. 15,000 earth's axis will point toward the constellation of Lyra, some 47° removed. The seasons will occur when earth is at positions in its orbit directly opposite to those locations where the seasons occur presently. An observer looking into the sky on a summer evening in A.D. 15,000 will see Orion shining brightly. This would be an alarming sight for today's observer, but no doubt because of the slowness of the change it will be a perfectly normal vista for an observer of that far-off time.

You recall that the sidereal year is the time required for the earth to revolve through 360°, and the tropical year of the seasons is the interval between two successive appearances of the sun at the vernal equinox. Since precession causes the equinox to drift westward—and since the apparent motion of the sun is eastward—the effect is that the vernal equinox meets the sun. Each year the equinox drifts westward through about 50 seconds of arc—this is enough to reduce by about 20 minutes the time for the sun to complete a passage from the vernal equinox around the zodiac and back again.

The amount of annual precession varies slightly from 50 seconds because the forces that cause the motion are not applied constantly. When the sun or moon is directly in line with earth's bulge there is no force applied. The sun crosses the celestial equator twice a year and the moon crosses it twice a month, and at these moments of crossing there will be no force affecting precession. In addition, there are variations in the orientation of the moon's orbit with respect to the ecliptic. All these factors affect precession by causing slight fluctuations in it. These are called *nutations*, after a Latin word meaning "to nod." The variations in the curve never amount to more than a fraction of a second of arc.

The poles of the earth wander in still another way. Very careful calculations of the latitude of places on the earth reveal that the earth shifts under the pole through a rather circular orbit having a diameter slightly more than one half second of arc. This is equal to sixty or seventy feet. This may be due to changes in the distribution of masses around the earth. Winds blow in different directions, air masses tend to be located at different places, high and low pressure areas travel various paths. There is an annual rhythm to this wandering of the poles. In addition there appears to be another component to the motion, one that has a period of 428 days, somewhat more than a year. This rhythm is probably a natural period of vibration of the earth that results from forces that tend to misshape it.

At the same time that the earth is rotating, revolving, precessing, and nutating, it is moving in other ways. The sun is not stationary in space. It moves among the stars and carries the entire solar system with it. Astronomers observing the stars in our vicinity have noticed that the stars appear to be receding from a region around the stars Vega and Delta Herculis. This would be the area located at about 18 hours right ascension and 34° north declination. All the stars in this region appear to be moving from one another. Sir William Herschel, an English astronomer who was a skilled stellar observer, reasoned that the general opening up of the sky in that area could be a result of our motion toward it. The situation is much the same as that experienced when you move toward a clump of trees. As you move closer to them the trees seem to move farther apart. The sun appears to be moving toward the eastern portion of the constellation Hercules at a velocity of twelve miles per second—some 43,000 miles an hour.

The sun is only one of billions of stars that comprise the Milky Way Galaxy. This galaxy of ours is big beyond belief—some 100,000 light years in diameter. The entire galaxy is rotating, spinnning around so that a complete turn is made in 200 million years. At the location of the solar system the velocity of rotation is 150 miles per second—more than 500,000 miles an hour.

You are on a planet that is rotating 1,000 miles an hour at the equator, revolving around the sun 66,000 miles an hour, drifting toward Hercules 43,000 miles an hour, and going around the center of the galaxy half a million miles per hour. And that's not all. The galaxy itself is moving through space. All galaxies appear to be moving away from all other galaxies at velocities that vary with the distance between them—the greater the distance, the greater the velocity. As seen from the most distant galaxies we may be moving through space at a velocity approaching the speed of light. As seen from galaxies that are closer, our velocity would be less.

We are well aware of some of the motions of our planet. Others do not register upon our senses at all. Their discovery and calculation have rested upon man's ability to make accurate measurements and intellectually, at least, to place himself at locations where he can "see" the planet in its entirety.

In a somewhat similar manner we are certainly aware of the gravity of the earth, or we certainly would be aware of it if suddenly there were no gravity at all. In the next chapter the force of gravity, some of the men who have investigated the force, and the knowledge of our planet that has been gathered through understanding gravity and its effects will be discussed.

4

GRAVITY AND THE EARTH'S SHAPE

THE VIEW THAT ancient man had of the world was extremely narrow. Furthermore, there was little inclination to explore beyond the limitations of one's senses. Their limited vista revealed none of the roundness of the earth and so it was inevitable that most men believed that the earth was flat. But in ancient days not everyone accepted this notion. There were certain individuals who would not believe what observations implied and who maintained, on the basis of logic alone, that the earth must be round. One of these men was Pythagoras, a Greek philosopher and teacher who, as early as the sixth century B.C., said that the earth is a sphere. Two hundred years later, Aristotle used observations to strengthen his belief in the roundness of the earth. Whenever a lunar eclipse occurred, he noticed that the edge of earth's shadow on the moon was curved. The curve was always an arc of a circle, and Aristotle concluded that only a spherical earth could produce such a shadow. Aristotle was right, of course, but the conclusion failed to convince most of his contemporaries as well as people who came after him. The part of the earth that they could see was flat, and so they assumed that the earth as a whole must be flat. They believed in the adage "seeing is believing."

When ships began to sail the open seas, the disappearance of a ship below the horizon seemed to ancient people proof that the earth was flat, for the ships appeared to have dropped off the edge of the world. They must have found it hard to explain how the ships that returned could have completed the journey after having dropped into oblivion. Had these ancient men watched more carefully they would have seen that a ship does not drop out of sight instantaneously. It disappears gradually; first the hull, followed by the superstructure, and finally the tops of the masts. The appearance of a ship also occurs gradually, first masts and then hull. Both observations are obvious. They can be explained by supposing that the earth is round. As Aristotle reported long ago, the limb (or edge) of the earth's shadow cast on the moon during the onset of a lunar eclipse is always curved, the arc of a circle. This is an effect of earth's roundness, for it is true that only a spherical object can cast a shadow of this shape regardless of its position. If the earth were any other shape—a cube or oval or flat surface—there would have been some time during an eclipse when the shadow would have been other than the curved arc of a circle.

High-flying airplanes and man-carrying satellites have enabled modern man to broaden his view. From the perspective now attainable he is able to see the earth's curvature directly, and so the most skeptical among us must accept that earth is indeed a sphere. Other observations have been made and lines of reasoning have been followed that provide further evidence of the true shape of the earth.

For example, let's assume that the earth is a flat surface. Let's also assume that the stars are very far away, as indeed they are. If you moved to the north or south on this flat surface, a star, Polaris for example, would always be at the same altitude above the horizon. However, repeated observations have shown that the altitude of Polaris changes as one moves to the north or south. For every seventy miles that the observer travels, the change is one degree.

Suppose a person at the equator were to observe Polaris. He would see the star on the northern horizon. When this person had moved seventy miles to the north, the star would be one degree above the horizon.

The change in altitude is directly proportional to the north-south distance traveled—one degree equals seventy miles. And this is always very nearly true as one moves north or south of his position, no matter where he is located. Since the relationship is true and always very nearly the same, the curve must be uniform and it must be an arc of a circle. The size of the circle can be found easily. We know there are 360° in a circle, and we know each degree represents a change of seventy miles, so 25,200 miles (70 miles × 360°) must be the circumference of the circle. This result is not much different from the distance around the earth as computed by other techniques.

In the latter part of the third century B.C. Eratosthenes, a Greek who was librarian at Alexandria, Egypt, during the Greek occupation of that land, observed the elevation of the sun from various locations. Not only did he show that the earth was round, but he also determined its size. At the city of Syene, now Aswan, in Upper Egypt, quite near to the Tropic of Cancer, one could observe that at the time of the summer solstice the sun stood directly overhead. The sun would be reflected from the surface of the water in a deep well. At the same time another observer could see that the situation was quite different at Alexandria, a city to the north on the shores of the Mediterranean Sea. Here the sun was found to be 7°15′ from the vertical. Assuming that the rays of the sun were parallel, Eratosthenes reasoned that the surface of the earth between Syene and Alexandria must be curved in an arc of 7°15′.

The distance between Syene and Alexandria was believed to be 5,000 stadia. The length of the stadium (a unit of measurement used by the Greeks) was derived from the length of an actual arena in Greece, probably 517 feet. The observed angle, 7°15′, is about one fiftieth of a complete circle (360°). Since the length of the arc was 5,000 stadia, then the distance all around the earth must be some fifty times greater—or 250,000 stadia. Using

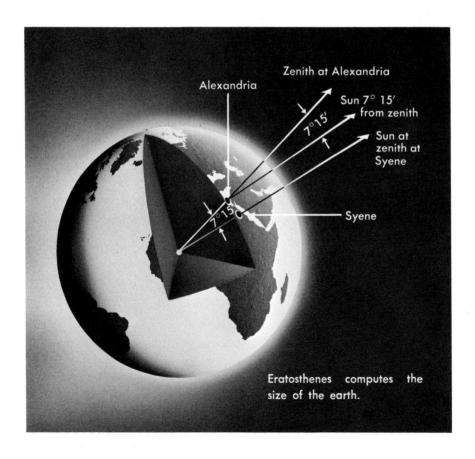

Eratosthenes computes the size of the earth.

517 feet as the length of a single stadium we find that the circumference of the earth as computed by Eratosthenes was nearly 24,500 miles. The figure is remarkably close to the results obtained by modern methods.

We cannot be certain if the distance between Syene and Alexandria was actually measured or not. Guesses and estimates may have been the most reliable data available. However, the procedure that Eratosthenes followed was sound. In fact, in the ninth century the Arabs used it to make their own measurement of the size of the earth. Apparently they measured off a distance on the surface sufficient to cause a change of one degree in the elevation or altitude of the sun. Once having done this, all they had to do was multiply that distance by 360. Whether or not the results of the Arabs were more accurate than those of the Greeks we shall never know, for we do not have any equivalent modern value for the units of measurement used by the Arabs. However, judging by the procedure they followed, it would seem that the ancient Arabs had a good idea about the size of the earth.

For some eight hundred years no further studies were made to learn the size of the earth. It was not until the early part of the seventeenth century that a professor, Willebrord Snell, of the University of Leyden in Holland, made extremely careful measurements of the surface of the earth to determine the equivalent value of the degree of latitude. He found it to be 66.73 miles, later corrected to 69.07 miles. This meant that the circumference of the earth would be 24,865 miles; the diameter would be 7,910 miles. This is very close to the figures accepted today, 7,926.68 miles for the equatorial diameter of the earth, and 7,899.98 miles for the polar diameter.

Later in the seventeenth century, investigators suspected that the earth was not a sphere, but was flattened at the poles and broadened at the equator. In 1671, the director of the Paris

Observatory sent an expedition to Cayenne, an island off French Guiana, situated 5° north of the equator. The purpose was to observe Mars when it was relatively close to the earth so that a more accurate determination of the distance of Mars from the sun could be made. Jean Richer, the leader of the expedition, carried with him a fine pendulum clock. He found that at Cayenne the clock lost 2 1/2 minutes in 24 hours—such a loss that he had to shorten the length of the pendulum by about one fourth inch to have it keep accurate time by the stars. Richer did not know the reason for this difference in the performance of the clock. But he may have suspected it occurred because the earth was not a perfect sphere. Near the equator the surface of the earth is farther from the center of the earth than are the polar regions, and gravitational force is less.

Some fifteen years later, Isaac Newton reasoned that the rotation of the earth would cause material to be piled up in the equatorial region. The shape of the earth, together with its rotation, would cause the value of gravity to increase from the equator to the poles. Now there was an answer to the puzzle of Professor Richer's pendulum. Since the equatorial region is farther from the axis of rotation than Paris, the force of gravity is less there than at Paris. This was the reason why Richer's pendulum clock lost time.

Here, too, was the explanation for precession of the equinoxes, discovered some eighteen hundred years earlier by Hipparchus. If the earth were a sphere, then forces of other objects upon the earth would be the same at all times and at all places. But since the earth was not a sphere, the moon and sun would exert a downward or upward force on the bulge of the earth. This attraction together with effects of earth's rotation enabled a full explanation of precession as discussed in the previous chapter.

The polar cross-section of the earth is an ellipse and its shape has been determined by many careful measurements made by different observers through the years. The need for accurate determinations of the shape and size of the earth became urgent in the seventeenth and eighteenth centuries, when more and more ships ventured farther into the open seas. The technique was the same as that which Eratosthenes had used hundreds of years earlier. North-south lines with lengths equivalent to one degree of latitude, or some part of a degree, were measured at different places around the earth and by different investigators. Repeatedly it was found that a degree of latitude is longer at the poles than it is at the equator. A degree of latitude is a small arc of a circle. Therefore, the size of the earth-sphere as implied from the measurement made at the poles would be greater than the size of the sphere as determined from the equatorial measurements. This is shown in the illustration. Obviously, the earth cannot be two different spheres at the same time. It cannot be a sphere at all. The measurements fit very nicely if we think of the

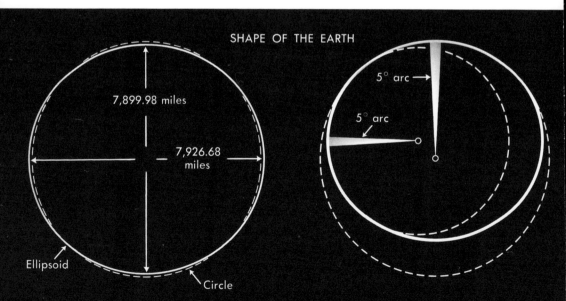

SHAPE OF THE EARTH

7,899.98 miles

7,926.68 miles

Ellipsoid

Circle

5° arc →

5° arc

The earth is an ellipsoid with the dimensions indicated.

Curvature of earth near poles is best fitted by a circle of larger circumference than the earth; along the equator, by a circle of

earth as an ellipsoid—the solid that is produced when an ellipse is rotated around its short axis.

Six measurements of the ellipsoid of the earth that have been widely used are given below:

Dimensions of ellipsoids:

		Equatorial Radius (Meter)	Polar Radius (Meter)	Flattening (Ratio of difference to the semi-major axis)
Fischer	1960	6,378,160	6,356,778	1/298.3
Hayford	1909	6,378,388	6,356,912	1/297
Clarke	1880	6,378,301	6,356,584	1/293.47
Clarke	1866	6,378,206	6,356,584	1/294.98
Bessel	1841	6,377,397	6,356,079	1/299.15
Everest	1830	6,377,276	6,356,075	1/300.8

The ellipsoid computed by J. F. Hayford of the U.S. Coast and Geodetic Survey, in 1909, is the one that is most widely used today. This ellipsoid gives a flattening of the earth of 1/297. The oblateness, or flattening, of the earth is obtained as indicated below:

$$\text{Oblateness} = \frac{\text{Equatorial radius} - \text{Polar radius}}{\text{Equatorial radius}}$$

$$\text{Oblateness (Hayford)} = \frac{6{,}378{,}388 - 6{,}356{,}912}{6{,}378{,}388}$$

$$\text{Oblateness} = \frac{21{,}476}{6{,}378{,}388} = \frac{1}{297}$$

The amount of flattening is so small that an observer looking at the earth from outer space would think he was observing a perfect sphere. Were the earth spinning faster, the flattening would be more noticeable. Jupiter and Saturn, both much larger than the earth, spin much faster. The flattening of these planets, 1/15 in the case of Jupiter and 1/10 in the case of Saturn, is obvious, even when they are viewed through a small telescope.

Precise measurements of satellite orbits, especially the orbit of Vanguard I—the small, grapefruit-sized satellite that was launched March 17, 1958—suggest strongly that the flattening of the earth should be 1/298.2 rather than 1/297. This means that the earth is flattened at the poles 250 feet less than previously supposed.

If the earth were perfectly spherical, the plane of a satellite orbit would always have the same orientation. But no orbit remains fixed. The planes of all satellite orbits rotate slowly around the axis of the earth because of earth's flattening. All satellite orbits precess.

Observations of a satellite are made regularly over a long period of time to determine the amount of precessing that occurs. From this knowledge, scientists can compute what the shape of the earth must be. As mentioned above, the amount of flattening appears to be less than previously believed.

In addition, the earth appears to be unsymmetrical—that is, the shape of the earth would not appear the same were it turned upside down. Mathematicians reached this conclusion because of measurements of changes in Vanguard's orbit. The average

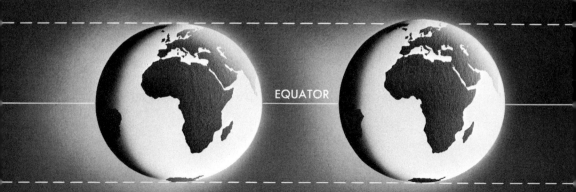

EQUATOR

The earth is not symmetrical as at left; the radius to the North Pole is about 50 feet longer than the radius to the South Pole, as shown at right.

distance of the orbit from earth's center decreases very slowly, about five miles a year. However, the minimum distance from earth's center varies between 4,367 and 4,373 miles. The swing from one distance to the other occurs regularly every eighty-two days. When this information is put into equations, the shape of the earth comes out about as shown in the illustration. The North Pole radius of the earth appears to be about fifty feet greater than the South Pole radius.

In 1963, in another effort to improve measurements of the size of the earth and distances from one place to another, a satellite with the code name Anna was launched. This gave geodesists, men concerned with mapping the earth, another nearby reference to use in their calculations. On signal, a light aboard Anna would flash. Sightings of the flashing light against background stars were made from two separate locations on the earth. By measuring at the two locations the angles between the light and the land surface, the distance between the two stations could be computed very accurately. The program continued for some time, but had to be terminated because the batteries to power the light wore down.

The same kind of investigation is now made using a laser beam, a very powerful beam of light that originates on the earth, strikes a satellite equipped with reflecting mirrors, and is returned to the stations. With laser beams, a lightweight satellite can be used, one that has no power difficulties at all. The reflected light makes just as good a reference as the light generated by the satellite itself.

Laser is a coined word made from the initial letters of "light amplification by stimulated emission of radiation." The light beam is very intense and, unlike light from other sources, it remains in a narrow beam, spreading only slightly. When it leaves the laser generator the beam has a diameter of one quarter inch. At the location of the satellite, some 200 miles above the earth, the beam has spread to about a four-mile width, considerably less than an ordinary light beam would spread. The reflectors aboard the satellite catch a small amount of the total beam and reflect it to earth. When it arrives, this reflected beam has a diameter of about one hundred yards. The time required for the round trip is about one hundredth of a second.

It is reasonable to expect that the laser technique for mapping the earth will continue to be developed.

However, the main interest of geodesists still remains to chart accurately the force of gravity all around the earth. Once this has been done, the shape of the earth can be computed with great precision. The total force of gravity is made up of several different factors. Some of these are: the force that would result if the earth were a perfect sphere, the effect caused by the flattening of the earth, the effect resulting from differences in the shape of the northern and southern hemispheres. The more data there are about such factors, the more reliable the findings become. We can expect that geodesists will continue their efforts to measure earth's gravity by utilizing satellites and so arrive at a fuller and more accurate picture of the shape of the earth.

Gravity

If you were to measure roughly the force of gravity at various locations around the earth you would find the results nearly the same. However, if one used a precise mechanism, the kind of pendulum clock that the Frenchman Jean Richer used, for example, the results would show differences. They would lead one to the conclusion that the earth is an oblate spheroid; an ellipsoid —the solid traced out by an ellipse turning about its minor axis. Yet, there would be small exceptions from the ellipsoidal shape.

Newton's law of gravitation is the basis for the study of earth's gravity. Newton stated that two bodies attract one another with a force directly proportional to the product of their masses and inversely proportional to the square of the distance between them. This means that if you double one of the masses, you double the force of attraction. And if you double the distance separating the two masses, the attraction between them will be one fourth as great; if you triple the distance, the attraction will be one ninth as great; and so on.

Gravity measurements made with a pendulum at different locations vary for several reasons—the mass of the material directly below the pendulum, or nearby, may vary; there may be differences in the distance from the pendulum to the center of the earth; or there may be differences in the centrifugal force of earth's rotation.

The swing of a pendulum is still a good measure of gravity. The length of time required for a swing to be completed changes with changes of gravity. By timing millions of swings, accurate measurements of gravity can be determined. The strength of earth's gravity can be measured to an accuracy of one part in fifty million.

An instrument that enables measurements to be made quickly is the gravimeter. This is a very delicate and sensitive spring scale. The pull of the earth causes a fine wire to be stretched, and the amount of stretching can be measured. Readings made with a gravimeter or with a pendulum are compared at the world standard station for gravity measurements located at the Helmert Tower in Potsdam, Germany.

Gravity is usually stated in g's, or acceleration of gravity. This tells us how rapidly an object would increase its rate of fall if it were falling free in a vacuum. The acceleration of gravity at earth's surface is 32 feet per second per second—or about 980 centimeters per second per second. This is usually written 32 ft/sec^2 or 980 cm/sec^2. If one were to drop a weight from a high building, it would fall 16 feet during the first second—remember that it has zero velocity at the start. At the end of second number two it will have fallen 64 feet. The object is moving faster at a steady rate of increase—32 feet per second per second. The fall during ten seconds may be represented as below:

| Time | | During That Second | | Total |
(Seconds)	Velocity	Increased Acceleration	Distance	Distance
1	32	32	16	16
2	64	32	48	64
3	96	32	80	144
4	128	32	112	256
5	160	32	144	400
6	192	32	176	576
7	224	32	208	784
8	256	32	240	1,024
9	288	32	272	1,296
10	320	32	304	1,600

Perhaps you can see the relationships in the preceding table more easily if we show them in a different way.

Total Distance	Distance During That Second	Increased Acceleration Each Second
16	48	32
64	80	32
144	112	32
256	144	32
400	176	32
576	208	32
784	240	32
1,024	272	32
1,296	304	32
1,600		

Readings made at various latitudes show that gravity increases as one moves closer to the poles—mainly because one is closer to the center of the earth and because centrifugal force becomes less. The gravity (g) readings at various latitudes are given below:

Latitude	g (cm/sec^2)
0°	978.049
15°	978.394
30°	979.388
45°	980.629
60°	981.924
75°	982.873
90°	983.221

These g values refer to the surface of the earth. As one moves away from the surface, the g readings will drop because one is moving farther from the center of the earth. Readings at various altitudes are given below:

Elevation (feet)	g (cm/sec^2)
0	978.049
5,000	977.579
10,000	977.108
15,000	976.639
20,000	976.169

If we were to continue out into space—all the way to the moon, for example—the acceleration of earth's gravity would drop considerably. At the moon's distance of 240,000 miles, earth's gravitational attraction is only 1/3,600 of what it is at the earth's surface—240,000 miles is 60 times 4,000 miles (earth's radius). Grav-

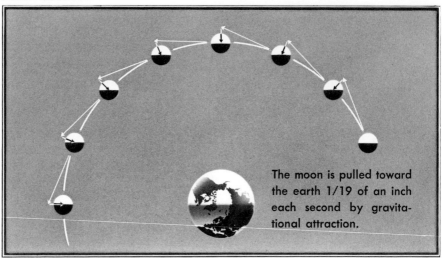

The moon is pulled toward the earth 1/19 of an inch each second by gravitational attraction.

ity is inversely proportional to the square of the distance, or $1/60^2$, or $1/3,600$. This means that an object should move toward the earth with an acceleration of $1/3600 \times 980$, or 0.272 cm/sec^2. If Newton's law is correct, this means that the moon is falling toward the earth at a velocity which is increasing 0.272 centimeters per second during each second. If one figured the extent of the fall for one day, he would find that the moon must fall some 6,300 miles toward the earth during twenty-four hours.

Certainly the moon is not approaching the earth at any such rate. If it were, it would have reached us long ago. By "falling" we mean that the moon is deflected by earth's gravitational attraction some 6,300 miles in twenty-four hours from a straight path—the path the moon would follow if earth's mass did not affect its course. Earth's gravitation keeps the moon in orbit. Similarly earth's gravitation affects the orbits of man-made satellites.

The Mass of the Earth

Sir Isaac Newton formulated his law of universal gravitation in 1687. Over a century was to go by before experimental proof of the law was obtained and before scientists succeeded in measuring this force. The feat was accomplished by Henry Cavendish (1731–1810), an English physicist; it was the last investigation he was to make in a lifetime of scientific discoveries. Cavendish attached a small metal sphere to each end of a rod and suspended the rod at its center by a fine wire. Two heavy lead spheres were brought close to the small ones. When this was done, the wire twisted ever so slightly. An outside force was applied so the small spheres were brought back to the original position. This force could be measured. Measurements made by Cavendish have been refined, so that the basis for measuring gravity is 666×10^{-10} dynes (you recall that 666×10^{-10} means you have 666 preceded by seven zeros—ten places to the right of the decimal—0.0000000666). This is the constant of gravity (G). It means that two 1-gram masses placed one centimeter apart attract each other with a force of 0.0000000666 dynes. A dyne is the force needed to move a one gram mass one centimeter per second. One cannot detect a single dyne with his senses—and the force we are talking about here is a minuscule fraction of a dyne.

By using the result of the Cavendish experiment we can compute the mass of the earth. When you're thinking about the mass of an object, it is easy to get mass confused with weight. Weight is really a force, the force which a given mass exerts on another mass. Your weight on the earth, for example, is the force which the entire mass of the earth exerts on you. Here on the earth we might express weight as in this equation:

$$W \text{ (Weight)} = M \text{ (Mass)} \times g \text{ (Acceleration of gravity)}$$

We already know that g is about 980 cm/sec², so the weight of a one-gram mass could be expressed in force units:

$$W = 1 \times 980$$
$$W = 980 \text{ (Dynes)}$$

The unit used here is the dyne. You recall it is a force which accelerates a one-gram mass one centimeter per second per second. The task of finding the mass of the earth appears quite formidable, but once you have a few facts it's as simple as putting a one-gram mass on a spring balance. The scale, of course, reads one gram, because the earth attracts the mass with a force of one gram, or 980 dynes. From Newton's law of universal gravitation we have:

$$F = \frac{G \times Mm}{d^2}, \text{ where}$$

F = 980 dynes
G = 666×10^{-10}
M = Mass of earth
m = Mass of one gram
d = Distance to center of earth
         in centimeters; 640,000,000

Now we can substitute these values in the equation.

$$980 = \frac{0.0000000666 \times M \times 1}{(640,000,000)^2}$$

When we solve the equation for M, we find that

$$M = 6 \times 10^{27} \text{ grams, or } 6.6 \times 10^{21} \text{ tons}$$

The mass of the earth is often called weight of the earth. This interchange of weight and mass has become commonplace, but one should keep in mind that weight is really a measure of the force exerted by an object on another body. If you sat on a spring scale on the moon, you would weigh one sixth of your earth weight. If you were on Jupiter, you would weigh 2.6 times your earth weight. But suppose that instead of using a spring scale you were to weigh yourself with a balance. The mass of material required to strike a balance will be exactly the same no matter if you are on the earth, the moon, or anywhere else. Mass does not change with changes in location. The value of 6×10^{27} grams for the earth will not change regardless of where the earth might be placed. It is a measure of earth's mass.

Another way of computing the mass of the earth involves forces between larger bodies.

Suppose we start with two masses. One of these weighs one pound and the other one ton. The two masses are placed so the distance between them is 1/1,000 of a mile. With sensitive instruments the force of attraction between the two masses is found to be 1/412,000,000 of one pound.

Let us move the one ton mass to the center of the earth. That distance would be 4 million times greater than 1/1,000 of a mile. (You recall that the radius of the earth is 4,000 miles. In one mile there are 1,000 thousandths, so in 4,000 miles there are 4 million thousandths.)

The force between two masses varies inversely with the *square* of the distance. This means that the force between the two masses will now be $4,000,000^2$ less than it was before. The force was 1/412,000,000 of a pound, so now it must be 1/412,000,000 $\times$ 1/16,000,000,000,000,000; or 1/6,592,000,000,000,000,000,000 (1/6.6 $\times 10^{21}$) of one pound. One ton at the center of the earth exerts a force of 1/6.6 $\times 10^{21}$ of a pound on a one pound mass on the surface. But we know that the actual force exerted by the earth on one pound at the surface is one pound. Therefore, the earth must be composed of 6,592,000,000,000,000,000,000 (6.6 $\times 10^{21}$) tons. Another way of saying this is, the mass of the earth is 6.6 $\times 10^{21}$ tons (6.6 $\times 10^{27}$ grams) since gravitation works as though all the mass of the earth were at earth's center.

When the mass of the earth is known we can determine its density. First the volume of the earth has to be computed.

Volume of earth $= 4/3 \, \pi \, r^3$

The radius of the earth in centimeters is 640,000,000. When the arithmetic is worked out the volume of the earth is found to be 1.083×10^{27} cubic centimeters. Divide volume into mass to obtain density.

$$\frac{5.975 \times 10^{27}\,\text{grams}}{1.083 \times 10^{27}\,\text{cubic centimeters}} = 5.5+\ \text{grams/cubic centimeter}$$

This means that the earth weighs about 5.5 times more than it would weigh if it were made of water. From data such as these, geologists can infer that the interior of the earth which we have never observed is made of identifiable kinds of materials, as discussed in the first chapter.

The knowledge and understanding of gravity that scientists have are far from complete. We can describe quite thoroughly the effects of gravitational force, but discussions of the nature of the force, its origin, and propagation ultimately run against blank walls. And so it is with earth's magnetism, which is discussed in the next chapter.

5

GEOMAGNETISM:
THE MAGNETOSPHERE
AND RADIATION BELTS

IN THE EARLY part of the eleventh century, Persians and Arabs developed thriving trade with the rest of the world, largely because they had learned how to safely navigate long voyages far from the sight of land. For centuries, they, and other ancient people, had used the stars to guide them. But the stars were no help when the sky was cloud covered. Many ships lost their way. But at the start of the eleventh century, magnetic compasses were used to point a course. They were effective day and night, in fair weather and foul. These early compasses indicated that the earth behaves as though it were a great magnet—attracting and repelling the compass needle.

Early compasses were lodestones—chunks of rich iron ore that had become magnetized by being in earth's magnetic field. The lodestones were either suspended or they were placed on a block of wood that floated in water. By the fourteenth century the magnetic compass had been refined. It had become a delicate instrument and was standard equipment on seagoing vessels. Ships could go on long voyages without losing their way. The compass made possible the Portuguese voyages of discovery and the great exploits of the Spanish armada and the British navy.

Early navigators used the sun and stars to determine their course and position. Even after the magnetic compass was developed, it was not relied upon completely. It was checked against the stars. While the compass tended to hold a direction, it became evident that the magnetic compass only rarely pointed to true north. The needle was deflected east or west of true north, and the amount of deflection changed as one moved from one part of the earth to another. Still, the earth did behave like a magnet in many ways.

Confirmation that the earth acted like a magnet was obtained in 1600 when William Gilbert, an English physician, published his findings concerning an investigation with lodestones. It was one of the earliest reports of an experimental investigation. Sir William knew from experiences on board ships that the behavior of a compass varied from the northern to the southern hemisphere. He also knew that a dip needle (a magnetic needle mounted to move vertically), pointed below the horizon in the northern hemisphere and above the horizon south of the equator. To investigate the behavior of a dip needle and find an explanation for it, Sir William constructed a sphere of lodestone to represent the earth and moved a dip needle around it. The needle behaved with the model as it did on the surface of the earth, and so William Gilbert therefore concluded that the earth is some-

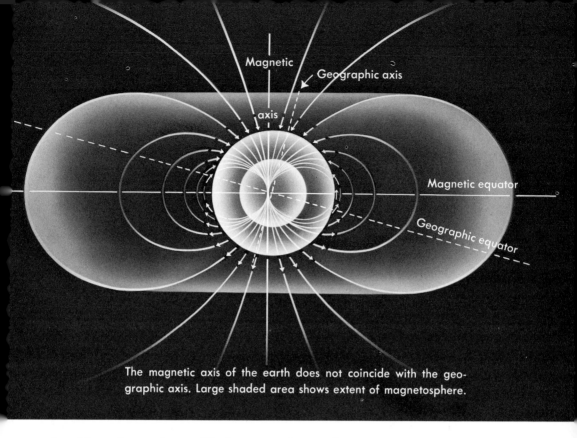

The magnetic axis of the earth does not coincide with the geographic axis. Large shaded area shows extent of magnetosphere.

what like a big sphere of lodestone; the earth is a great magnet.

William Gilbert supposed that the interior of the earth was magnetized in some way, although he was unable to explain how or why. Later this belief was refined, and men believed that metals within the earth were arranged in a bar; they thought that the earth was a great bar magnet. The poles of the magnet came near the surface in the north and south, the lines of force emerging through the surface and into space. The idea was quite logical, especially when you consider that at the time magnetism could be explained only in a very crude fashion. The earth definitely does have north and south magnetic poles, but presently geophysicists believe there is no bar within the earth. Actually, the magnetic axis does not pass through the center of the earth as had been supposed. The magnetic north pole is at about 70°

north latitude and 100° west longitude and the magnetic south pole at about 68° south latitude and 143° east longitude. Obviously, the poles are not directly opposite one another. The magnetic axis misses the center of the earth by quite a bit.

When we speak of a compass we say the north pole of the compass points toward the north pole of the earth. Such a situation cannot actually exist, for *unlike* poles attract each other. Therefore, to be accurate, one should call the end of a magnet that points toward the north, the *north-seeking* pole. The opposite end of the compass should be referred to as the *south-seeking* pole.

There are several reasons why earth's magnetism cannot be explained by supposing there is a great bar magnet below the surface around which the earth turns. In the first place, if you heat a magnet sufficiently, the metal becomes demagnetized. Temperatures below the surface of the earth are more than sufficient to destroy any magnetism that a metal might possess. The axis of earth's magnetic field is not the same as the axis around which the earth turns. There is a difference of several hundred miles between the locations of the geographic and magnetic poles. Furthermore, the pattern of earth's magnetic field changes appreciably and the changes occur within a relatively short time. There can be only one explanation for these variations and for these rapid changes. The interior of the earth, where magnetism is generated, cannot be solid, for the changes are too rapid to occur in a solid. There has to be some motion, internal movements of great masses of material. There has to be a state of continual change.

Contrary to the belief held by many, earth's magnetic field is very weak—several hundred times smaller than that between the ends of an ordinary horseshoe magnet. The magnetic field is not only weak, it is also irregular. Around the north and south mag-

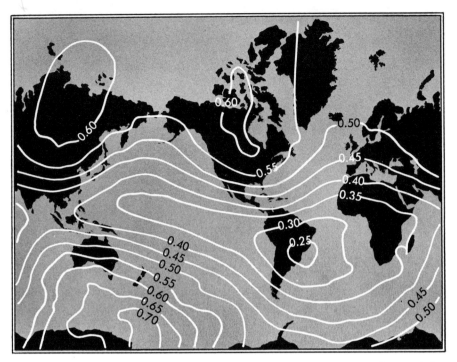

Map of magnetic intensity around the world. Values are in oersteds, a small unit of intensity.

netic poles the force is greatest. At the magnetic equator, about midway between the poles, the force of magnetism drops very low as shown in the illustration.

If one were to travel over the surface of the earth with a dip needle, the angle that the needle makes with the surface of the earth would change. As one neared the magnetic north pole, the north-seeking end would move closer and closer to 90°. Also, if one moved from place to place on the surface of the earth while carrying an ordinary compass, he would find that the needle would rarely point toward true north. It would point toward the magnetic north pole, which does not coincide with geographic

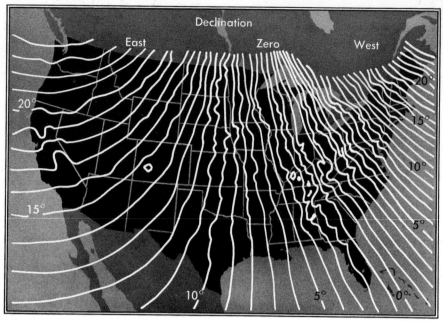

Lines of equal magnetic declination.

north. The difference between geographic and magnetic north is called magnetic declination. The magnetic declinations for the United States are shown on the map above. Declination in a given area changes continually. For example, in the vicinity of New York magnetic declination is increasing by one degree in something less than sixty years.

Long-period changes may be quite extreme, as shown on page 123. Notice that in London declination was some 12° east in 1576 and by 1823 it had become almost 25° west. During the same time the dip needle varied by about 5°.

Studies of the magnetization of rocks—the manner in which magnetized particles are arranged—enable geophysicists to infer movements of the earth's magnetic field that have occurred through millennia. Apparently the north pole has wandered somewhat as shown in the illustration on page 123. From studies

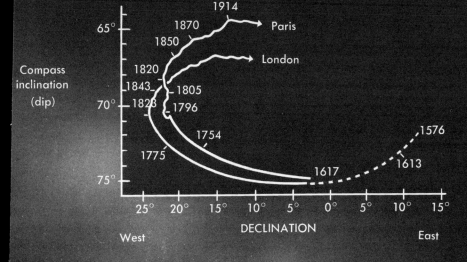

Changes in declination and dip at Paris and London for over three centuries are shown above. The heavy line (below) roughly traces wandering of the magnetic north pole, as determined by magnetic patterns in rocks.

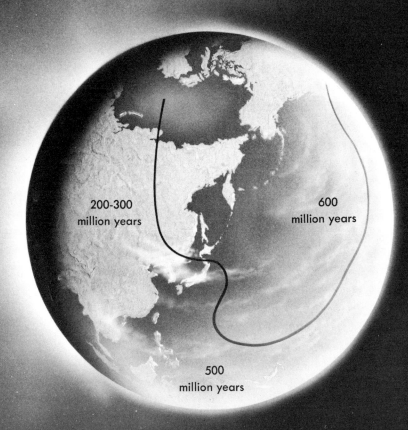

200-300
million years

600
million years

500
million years

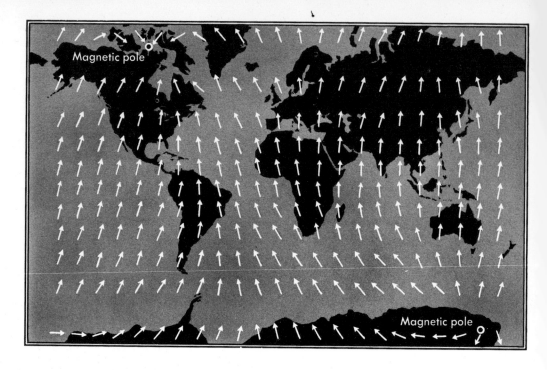

In the upper map we see the ideal dipole field which is made of two parts—a regular magnetic field and an irregular field. The lower map shows only the irregular field.

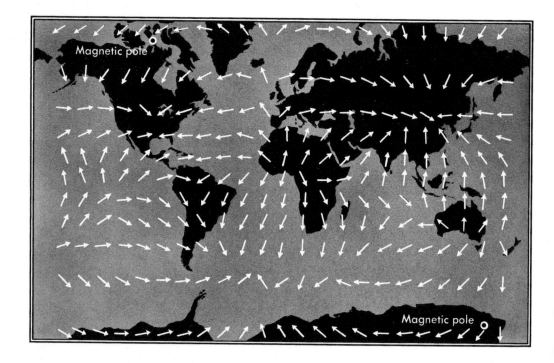

of these magnetic fossils (the magnetized particles in rocks) it appears that during the Tertiary Period (1 million to 60 million years ago) the north and south geomagnetic poles reversed positions many times. This conclusion, reached after studying layer upon layer of lava flow, is not shared by all researchers. Some believe that changes in the positions of the magnetized particles might have been produced by causes other than reversals of earth's magnetic fields.

Earth's magnetic field appears to be a combination of two magnetic fields. There is the main field which results when one assumes the earth acts like a fixed and unchanging bar magnet. This ideal field—smooth, even, and unbroken—is called the dipole field. The assumption is that the magnetic axis passes through earth's center and the poles are at opposite locations on the earth. Referred to as the geomagnetic poles, they are at latitude 79° N, longitude 70° W and latitude 79° S, longitude 110° E. The geomagnetic poles are the poles of the dipole field and are not the same as the magnetic poles—these being the places where a dip needle stands vertical to the surface.

The illustration of a dipolar magnetic field shows the way the north-seeking end of a compass needle points. Notice that the effect is quite smooth and regular. The lower diagram shows what happens when a uniform north-south field is subtracted from the total observed field. Apparently, there are two fields involved in the dipole field. The problem is to find ways of explaining how these two different fields originate.

The Causes of Magnetism

More than a hundred years ago Karl Friedrich Gauss, a German physicist, showed that the magnetic field must be produced inside the earth. Today, few would doubt that magnetism is produced inside the earth and that it is the result of electric currents produced by motions of great masses of material. It is common knowledge that an electric current generates a magnetic field. And the field may be produced in a bar of iron; or it may be produced in a gas or some other fluid. This is the essence of the study called magnetohydrodynamics.

We must first assume that within the earth there are electric currents. The currents may have been originated by chemical reactions or by temperature differences which produced a voltage between the poles and the equator—one volt would be more than enough. Or there might be a dynamo effect involving the core of the earth and earth's mantle.

A dynamo converts energy of motion into electrical energy. A very simple dynamo was developed by Michael Faraday (1791–1867), an English chemist and physicist who is often referred to as the "father of electricity." Faraday spun a disk of copper supported over a bar magnet by a spindle. An electric current was generated. The bar magnet might be replaced with an electric

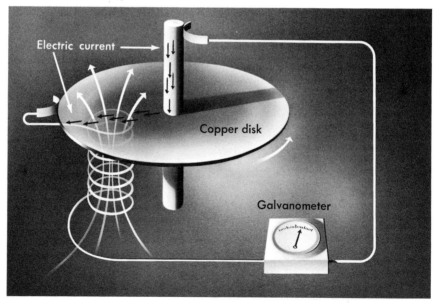

Electric current

Copper disk

Galvanometer

When a copper disk is turned above a coil of wire,
an electric current is generated.

coil. If we start with a current in the coil, an electric current will be produced in the copper disk just as above. If the current produced in the disk is fed back to the coil, the system is self contained—as long as the disk turns. Current is produced and the coil is electrified.

The Faraday disk cannot maintain itself very long because the metals offer high resistance to electricity. If the disk were made of a material that as a conductor was a thousand times better than copper or if the disk were spun very fast, the system would maintain itself. Another way to make the system maintain itself would be to make the disk larger—the larger the disk, the better it should work. If we could make a disk several miles in diameter it would maintain a current even if it turned very slowly. If the disk were as large as the earth it would work even if it barely moved.

Let's see how all this applies to the earth. We know that the earth has a fluid core that is 4,316 miles in diameter. Being liquid, it is possible for the core to be in motion with respect to the solid mantle of the earth. Furthermore, the core is probably made of iron or a nickel-iron alloy and so will conduct electricity. The core is exactly right for a Faraday-type dynamo.

From changes in the earth's magnetic field we can determine that the material in the core moves about a hundredth of an inch a second. As yet, we do not know the source of the energy for these motions. Some scientists believe that convection currents due to differences in temperature provide the necessary energy. Others think that slight variations in chemical composition (density) may set up motions that provide the energy. No matter what the source of the energy may be, we do know that the amount needed to maintain motion of particles in the core is exceedingly small.

Eddies that are rather limited in area are very likely produced

A circular electric current (black arrows), which produces earth's magnetic field, may be driven by smaller eddies of current.

by the dynamo process. Just where the eddies will be produced one cannot say. However, we do know that the general magnetic field which is made up of these eddies is not highly changeable as a whole. Apparently the general field can have many small and unpredictable variations within it without being changed itself.

Support of belief in the dynamo-effect in the earth has come from observations of magnetic fields in some sixty different stars. Stars rotate, and the gases of which they are made are good conductors of electricity. The magnetic fields of stars change rapidly. This observation and all other observations of the magnetic properties of stars lead to the conclusion that the effects are produced by the dynamo process. This same process, magnetohydrodynamics, appears to be the one that produces the magnetic effects we experience on this planet.

Radiation Belts

One of the earliest discoveries made by man-made satellites was also one of the most spectacular, and led to a surprising extension of our knowledge of earth's magnetic field. In 1958 Explorers I and III passed through vast fields of charged particles—protons and electrons—that were trapped by earth's magnetic field. Determination of the outer boundaries of these belts of radiation defined quite clearly the extent of the geomagnetic field. The magnetic lines of force may extend hundreds of thousands of miles into space, becoming weaker with distance, and finally fading away altogether. However, the boundary within which the field is clear-cut and effective is much closer to earth, probably not exceeding fifty thousand miles. The volume surrounding the earth and containing the magnetic field is called the magnetosphere. It is a region of much puzzlement. Auroras, magnetic storms that interfere with radio communication, and the faint light of the evening sky called airglow all seem to have origins in this region, and all of these are phenomena that are poorly understood. Even though millions of observations have been made by satellites, probes, and other rocket-borne devices, we are still quite ignorant of the composition of the region and the manner in which particles comprising the region interact.

The magnetosphere is not a smooth, uniform belt as often represented, but quite uneven and irregular. Streams of particles from the sun (the solar wind) push the lines of magnetic force together, compressing them on the sunlit side of the earth to about one half of their extent of some forty-five thousand miles that prevails during intervals of low solar activity. On the dark side of the earth, we cannot yet say how far the magnetosphere extends, but sixty to seventy thousand miles seems a reasonable estimate. The magnetosphere is three-dimensional, having a ra-

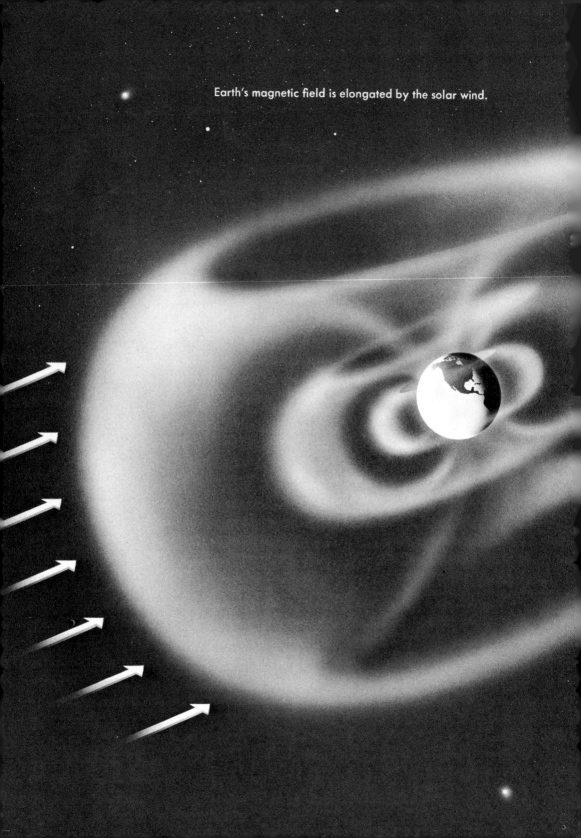

Earth's magnetic field is elongated by the solar wind.

Routes of protons and electrons trapped in earth's magnetic field
drift around earth.

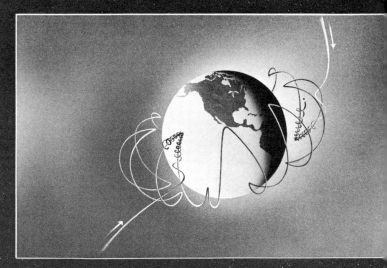

dius of tens of thousands of miles at right angles to a line connecting the earth and sun.

The earth, as well as the other inner planets, may have a trailing tail of gases millions of miles long. The tails would point away from the sun much as do the tails of comets, and for the same reasons.

The tails of comets are made of materials that have been blown away from the comet head by the solar wind. The tail of the earth is an elongation of the earth's magnetic field. The central part is flattened and jammed with electrons. They are held in by the

Planets may have long "tails" produced when sub-atomic particles that are held by magnetic fields are pushed away by the solar wind.

H. K. WIMMER

magnetic walls of the tail itself. Instruments aboard satellites have detected the electrons out to 120,000 miles. It is believed that as investigations continue to greater distances we shall find that planets as far out as Saturn possess tails. A reason for this belief is the fact that the tails of comets persist to about that distance. Beyond Saturn the solar wind appears unable to push the particles from the head, and the tail collapses. If the tails of planets are produced by the solar wind then they should also disappear at that same distance.

Some scientists think earth's tail may extend beyond Pluto, forty times the earth's distance from the sun. If this should be true, then the tails of Mercury and Venus, if they do exist, should extend beyond the earth, and we should pass through them. More research and observations are needed to gather information about the tails of planets. However, they must be related to earth's magnetic field and the changes that occur in it.

Protons and electrons of rather low energy are found throughout the magnetosphere, captured by the lines of force. However, there are many localized regions that hold high-energy particles.

About two thousand miles above the magnetic equator, the region midway between the geomagnetic poles, there is a belt of high-energy protons. About ten thousand miles out there is a belt of high-energy electrons that girdles the equator. These are the Van Allen belts, named after James A. Van Allen, the physicist whose experiment aboard Explorer I discovered the radiation particles that envelop the earth. At first scientists could not believe that Explorer had really found high-energy particles, for their existence had not been expected. The instruments aboard the satellite were designed to measure low-energy particles. But every experiment aboard subsequent satellites indicated the same conclusions. Some of the satellites that confirmed the finding were Explorer IV, the three U.S. moon probes: Pioneers I, III, and IV, the second and third earth satellites launched by the Russians, and the first Russian moon vehicle.

The Geiger counters aboard Explorer I, which was launched in January 1958, were designed to measure cosmic rays at high altitudes. But the radiation level was much too high to have been caused by cosmic particles, and so another explanation had to be found. It was suggested and later proved to be true that earth's magnetic field captured charged particles and held them in great belts. High-energy protons in the outer belt spiral around magnetic force lines in great loops some three thousand miles in diameter. Low-energy protons are held more tightly by earth's magnetic field. They spiral in loops having a diameter of only about a hundred miles. Electrons, having little mass, are held even tighter. The loops in which low-energy electrons spiral may have a diameter little more than one mile. The trapped particles spiral around the magnetic lines of force, bouncing back and forth from one polar region to the other in only a few seconds. Those particles that are not trapped probably leak into the atmosphere or are thrown into space. As the particles move along the lines of force, they drift around the earth. Electrons drift to the east, protons to the west, completing the journey around the earth in a few minutes or a few hours. There is little, if any, trapping beyond 75° latitude on the sunlit side of the earth, and 70° latitude on the dark side. Since these are the regions where auroras occur many physicists believe there is a direct relationship between the auroras and the polar boundaries of the magnetosphere. Above the polar region, space is quite empty of radiation particles. These regions are corridors through which unimpeded access to outer space is possible.

A small part of the radiation in the inner belt (less than one percent) is made of high-energy protons. The rest of the radiation is due to electrons. The particle flux is high. Flux is the product of the density and the velocity of the particles. In the outer Van Allen belt the flux may vary by a factor of ten in less than twenty-four hours. In the inner belt, the flux remains quite steady, requiring about a year to change by a factor of only three.

Because the particles in the two regions behave differently, it was logical to suppose that the particles might originate in different ways. Cosmic radiation could be the source of the particles that comprise the inner belt—for cosmic radiation is quite steady. The rapid changes in the outer belt would indicate that they have an abundant and changeable source. Studies show a relationship between the flux of particles and the level of sun activity, indicating that the sun may be the direct source of these particles.

The outer Van Allen belt posed problems in the early days of investigation. Some people suspected that there were multitudes of low-energy electrons in the region, and others believed that there were smaller numbers of particles but that each particle contained considerable energy. The problem was not solved until 1961 with the flight of Explorer XII. This probe found that there are at least two quite distinct regions in the outer belt. In the outer part there are electrons that move at very high velocities. Even though there are relatively few electrons, their high velocity produces a high flux. You recall that flux is the product of particle density and velocity. The electrons contain more energy than that given them by the sun, meaning that energy must be added to them in some fashion. While the full explanation is not known, perhaps earth's magnetic field, which fluctuates during storms, would set up a pulsing action. This would pump the electrons along, speeding them up to higher velocities.

In addition to the high-energy electrons in the outer belt, there is also a background of low-energy particles. The energy of these electrons is measured in tens of thousands of electron volts rather than in millions.

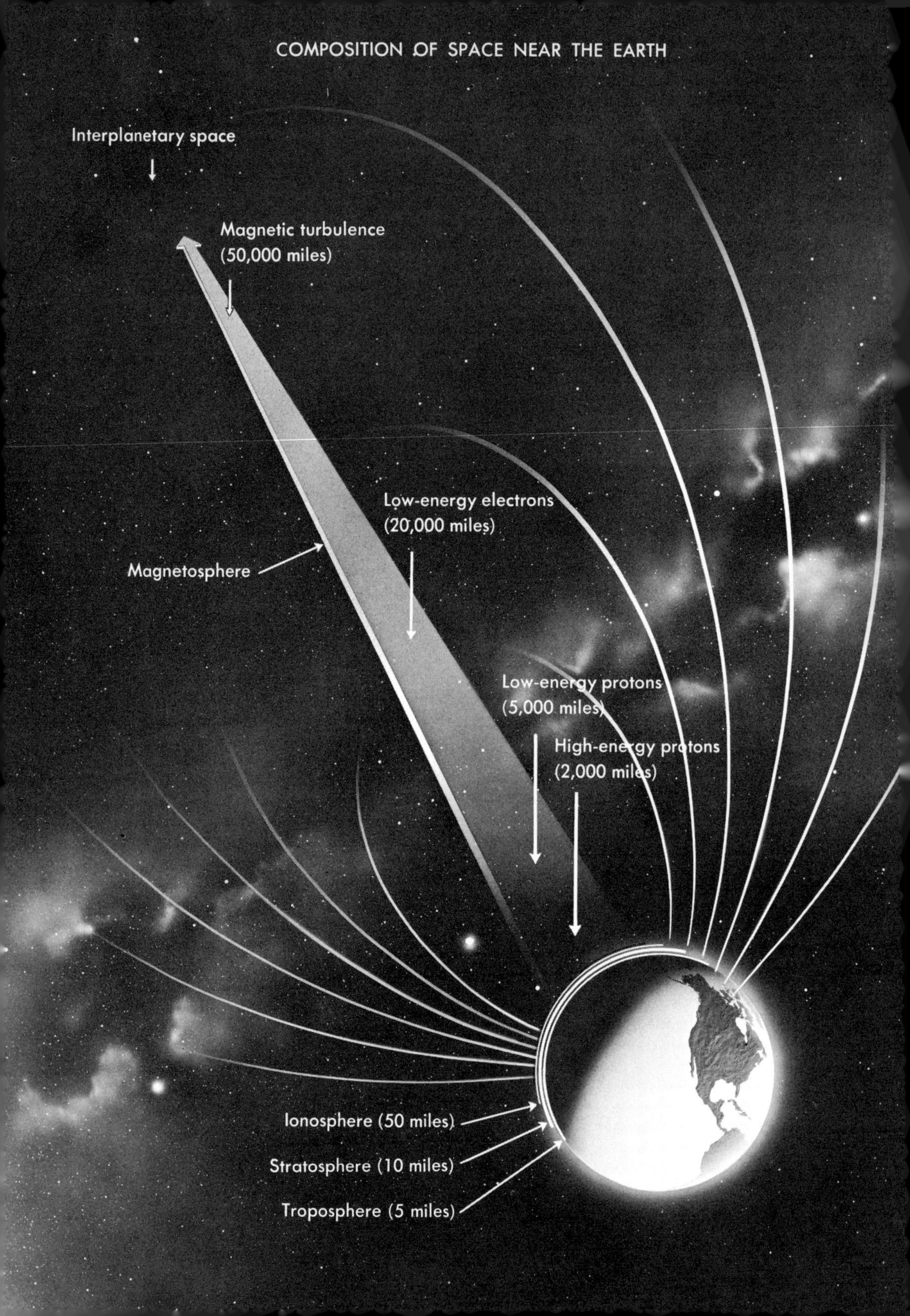

COMPOSITION OF SPACE NEAR THE EARTH

Interplanetary space

Magnetic turbulence
(50,000 miles)

Low-energy electrons
(20,000 miles)

Magnetosphere

Low-energy protons
(5,000 miles)

High-energy protons
(2,000 miles)

Ionosphere (50 miles)

Stratosphere (10 miles)

Troposphere (5 miles)

Auroras

The northern lights, aurora borealis, and the southern lights, aurora australis, appear to be closely related to earth's magnetic field. They occur in a great ring around the magnetic poles, and at elevations up to almost seven hundred miles, although most displays are observed at lower altitudes.

Protons and electrons moving along magnetic lines of force interact. The electron is captured by a proton. As the electron changes position within the atom, energy is liberated. Some of this energy is in the form of visible light. The nuclear particles may also collide with ions of various kinds in the upper atmosphere. Capture of electrons by certain ions, and the changing of electrons from one location within the ion to another releases energy of many wavelengths within the visible range, accounting for the beautiful soft arrays of color that we see in the auroras.

The particles responsible for auroras appear to originate in the sun. A day or so after a solar flare near the center of the solar disk we can expect to see aurora displays, and to experience disturbances in earth's magnetic field. Also, particles may escape from solar prominences and from streams of gases that arise from the solar corona. In any event, auroras and solar activity do appear to be related. However, every night an aurora appears somewhere in the auroral zone. We cannot expect that there must be some unusual solar occurrence to produce every aurora.

Early in the Space Age after the radiation belts that surround earth were discovered, scientists suggested that auroras were produced by particles spilling from those regions. Van Allen suggested a "leaky bucket" explanation. The outer radiation belt, the bucket, trapped particles from the sun. It could hold just so many particles. When more arrived, the bucket ran over. The particles spilled toward earth, mostly down through the auroral zones.

Later experiments revealed that the particles that were causing auroras and magnetic disturbances possessed varying amounts of energy. There could not be a simple spilling-over process. If the outer belt acted as a bucket, there had to be some way of speeding up the particles.

In 1960 Pioneer V flew through a cloud of particles that had been ejected from the sun. There were a vast number of particles, but the energy level was low. A few days later the same cloud of particles was encountered near the earth by another satellite. Now the energy level was a thousand times greater. The particles had been accelerated by some force near the earth.

Other observations led researchers to the conclusion that the outer belt could not be a bucket that spilled over occasionally. The number of particles involved in observed aurora displays would have drained the bucket quickly—there just weren't enough particles, unless the supply was constantly replenished.

Some scientists suggest that instead of the outer belt being a leaky bucket, it should be considered a "splash catcher." Low-energy particles from the sun, or particles that have been trapped in earth's environment for millenia, are speeded up in some way and rush to the earth in the auroral zones. Tremendous amounts are involved. Some few of the particles do not reach the earth. These are the ones that are captured and become part of the outer radiation belt.

Scientists are a long way from fully understanding the sources of particles, as well as the manner in which they are speeded up. We have known about the existence of the Van Allen belts only since 1958. Although hundreds of thousands of observations have been made, we still need considerably more information before the composition of the belts is known and before we comprehend the main factors that affect the particles and the manner in which they move and interact.

Whistlers

Another interesting phenomenon that is related to earth's magnetic field is the whistlers. These are whistlelike sounds that one may hear on a radio. The whistles start out high-pitched and rapidly descend to lower pitches.

Apparently whistlers originate in flashes of lightning. If your A.M. radio is turned on, you can hear heavy static shortly after you see a flash of lightning. When a flash of lightning occurs around five hundred miles away, a whistler will follow the crash. In rapid succession other whistlers may be heard, each fainter and of longer duration than the previous one.

Radio waves produced by lightning travel outward into space, following curved lines of the earth's magnetic field. The waves

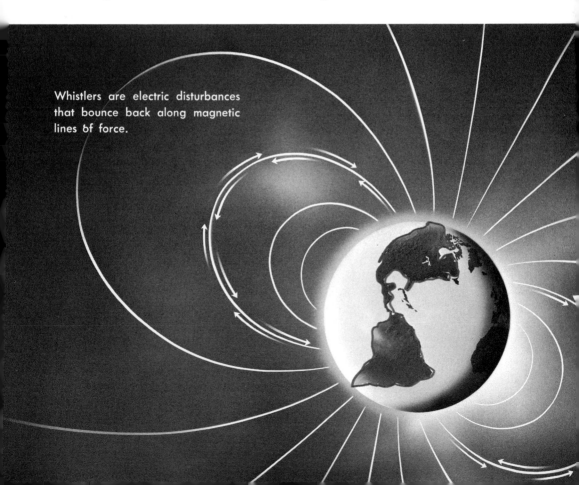

Whistlers are electric disturbances that bounce back along magnetic lines of force.

travel all the way to the opposite location on the earth, and then bounce back to the starting point.

Whistlers occur only in the middle latitudes. Near the equator the travel times are too short for them to develop, and near the poles the intervals are too great. Data about whistlers provide physicists with clues for measuring and mapping the earth's magnetic field, as can be implied from the illustration.

As you read this book you may have been surprised to discover that on the one hand we know quite a bit about this earth of ours, but on the other hand there are many questions that remain to be answered. Of all the planets of the solar system, ours is the only one that lends itself to firsthand investigations. Planetary probes to Venus and Mars gather data via long-distance automation. Delicate and highly varied measurements and investigations are extremely difficult and elusive. Here on earth we can apply tools and techniques in a manner that is simple and direct. Still, much remains to be learned about Planet Number Three. We are still far from understanding the nature of earth's magnetism and gravity; the shape of the earth and locations of islands and continents must be refined; slight variations in motions of the earth must be measured accurately and, it is hoped, explained.

The research scientist who seeks out an understanding of some small facet of the universe uncovers new problems as he solves the problem that started his investigation. This is as it should be, for if scientists have learned any single fact, it is that this world of ours is most complex. Its understanding challenges man's intellect, a challenge that we are confident young people will accept.

Some Facts About the Earth

DISTANCE FROM THE SUN .... mean 92,900,000 miles
aphelion 94,500,000 miles
perihelion 91,400,000 miles

VELOCITY OF ROTATION

Latitude	Feet per second
0°	1,525
30°	1,322
60°	765
90°	0

VELOCITY OF REVOLUTION .... mean 97,680 ft/sec (18.5 mps)
July 3—96,100 ft/sec
(aphelion)
Jan 3—99,300 ft/sec
(perihelion)

ECCENTRICITY OF ORBIT 0.017

DISTANCE AROUND ORBIT .... 683,942,855 miles

SOLAR MOTION TOWARD HERCULES
(R.A. 18^h 0^m; DECL. +28°) .... 12 mps (4 a.u./yr)

VELOCITY OF GALACTIC ROTATION AT
EARTH'S LOCATION .... 150 mps

LENGTH OF SIDEREAL DAY .... 0.9972696 mean solar days
23^h 56^m 4.09^s of mean solar time

SIDEREAL SECOND .... 1/86,400 of a sidereal day

SOLAR DAY .... 1.0027379 sidereal days
24^h 3^m 56.556^s of sidereal time

HOURS OF SUNLIGHT AT VARIOUS LATITUDES

Latitude	Maximum	Minimum
0°	12^h 5^m	12^h 5^m
20°	13^h 18^m	10^h 53^m
30°	14^h 2^m	10^h 10^m
40°	14^h 58^m	9^h 16^m
50°	16^h 18^m	8^h 0^m
60°	18^h 45^m	5^h 45^m
67.7°	24^h 0^m	0^h 0^m

LENGTH OF DAY/NIGHT IN POLAR LATITUDES

Latitude	Daylight	Darkness
70°	70 days	55 nights
80°	137 days	123 nights
90°	189 days	176 nights

LENGTH OF THE MONTH

Synodic (from new moon to new moon) 29^d 12^h 44^m 2^s.8

Sidereal (as measured by the stars) 27^d 7^h 43^m 11^s.5

TROPICAL YEAR (YEAR OF THE SEASONS) .... 365^d 5^h 48^m 45^s.975

SIDEREAL YEAR .... 365^d 6^h 9^m 9^s.740

(31,558,149.5 seconds)

(3.155 × 10^7)

DATES WHEN SEASONS BEGIN

Northern Hemisphere		Southern Hemisphere
Spring	March 20 or 21	Autumn
Summer	June 21 or 22	Winter
Autumn	September 23	Spring
Winter	December 22	Summer

LENGTHS OF SEASONS

Northern Hemisphere		Southern Hemisphere
Spring	92^d 19^h	Autumn
Summer	93^d 15^h	Winter
Autumn	89^d 20^h	Spring
Winter	89^d 0^h	Summer

OBLIQUITY OF ECLIPTIC (ANGLE BETWEEN ECLIPTIC AND EQUATOR) .... 23° 26′ 44″.84

VELOCITY OF ESCAPE AT SURFACE .... 6.95 mps

VOLUME .... 1,083,320,000,000 cu km

(1.083 × 10^9 km^3)

(1.083 × 10^{27} cm^3)

259,000 million cubic miles

SURFACE AREA .... 510,101,000 square kilometers

(510 × 10^6 km^2)

196,950,000 square miles

WEIGHT OF THE ATMOSPHERE .... 5,000,000,000,000,000 tons

(5 × 10^{15} tons)

MASS 6,600,000,000,000,000, 000,000

tons (6.6 × 10^{21} tons)

(6 × 10^{27} grams)

MASS OF EARTH COMPARED TO MASS OF
   THE SUN 1/332,488
DENSITY 5.52
ALBEDO (REFLECTIVITY OF THE SURFACE) 0.39
OBLATENESS 1/297
RADIUS .... Equatorial 6,378,388 meters
                                             3,936.34 miles
                                       Polar 6,356,912 meters
                                          3,949.99 miles
MAGNETIC POLES .... North magnetic dip pole:
                                       lat. 70° N., long. 100° W.
                                       South magnetic dip pole:
                                       lat. 68° S., long. 143° E.
                                       Geomagnetic north pole:
                                         lat. 79° N., long. 70° W.
                                         Geomagnetic south pole:
                                         lat. 79° S., long. 110° E.
INCLINATION OF MAGNETIC AXIS .... 11°.4 to the axis of rotation

MAJOR ELEMENTS COMPOSING THE EARTH, WATER, AND LAND

Element	Percent by weight
oxygen	49.5
silicon	25.8
aluminum	7.5
iron	4.7
calcium	3.4
sodium	2.6
potassium	2.4
magnesium	1.9
hydrogen	0.9
titanium	0.6

FURTHER READING

Abell, George. *Exploration of the Universe.* New York: Holt, Rinehart & Winston, 1964.

Asimov, Isaac. *The Double Planet.* New York: Abelard-Schuman, 1960.

Cromie, William J. *Exploring the Secrets of the Sea.* New York: Prentice-Hall, 1962.

Engel, Leonard, and the Editors of *Life. The Sea.* New York: Time, Inc.

Flammarion, Camille. *The Flammarion Book of Astronomy.* New York: Simon and Schuster, 1964.

Gamow, George. *A Planet Called Earth.* New York: Viking, 1963.

Hoyle, Fred. *Frontiers of Astronomy.* New York: Harper, 1955.

Marshack, Alexander. *The World in Space.* New York: Thomas Nelson and Sons, 1958.

Rudaux, Lucien, and De Vaucouleurs, G. *Larousse Encyclopedia of Astronomy.* New York: Prometheus Press, 1959.

Scientific American, editors of: *The Planet Earth.* New York: Simon and Schuster.

Spilhaus, Athelstan. *Satellite of the Sun.* New York: Viking, 1958.

Strahler, Arthur N. *The Earth Sciences.* New York: Harper & Row, 1963.

Stumpff, Karl. *Planet Earth.* Ann Arbor: University of Michigan Press, 1959.

Whipple, Fred. *Earth, Moon and Planets.* Cambridge: Harvard University Press, 1963.

Wyatt, Stanley. *Principles of Astronomy.* Boston: Allyn and Bacon, 1964.

INDEX

ABOUT THE AUTHOR

Dr. Franklyn M. Branley is well known as the author of many excellent science books for young people of all ages. He is also co-editor of the Let's-Read-and-Find-Out science books.

Dr. Branley is Astronomer and Assistant Chairman of the American Museum-Hayden Planetarium in New York City. He is Director of Educational Services for the Planetarium, where popular courses in astronomy, navigation, and meteorology are given for people of all ages.

Dr. Branley holds degrees from New York University, Columbia University, and the State University of New York College at New Paltz. He lives with his family in Woodcliff Lake, New Jersey.

ABOUT THE ILLUSTRATOR

Helmut K. Wimmer was born in Munich, Germany, and came to the United States in 1954. He immediately joined the Hayden Planetarium where he is a staff artist. Mr. Wimmer has illustrated many books on astronomy for young people.

He is also a sculptor and makes architectural models in his free time. He lives in New Jersey with his wife and children.